Free Schools

By Jonathan Kozol

Free Schools

Jonathan Kozol

Houghton Mifflin Company Boston

Second Printing c

Copyright © 1972 by Jonathan Kozol
All rights reserved. No part of this work may be
reproduced or transmitted in any form by any means,
electronic or mechanical, including photocopying
and recording, or by any information storage
or retrieval system, without permission in
writing from the publisher.
ISBN: 0-395-13606-7
Library of Congress Catalog Card Number: 73-179836
Printed in the United States of America

One hears more frequently now of parents banding together, finding teachers, and starting little schools . . . There are no signs that a movement exists, but there are many signs that one might . . .

— George Dennison, 1969

TO MRS. EDWARD BURNS
BLACK WOMAN OF STRENGTH AND LOVE

ACKNOWLEDGMENTS

Thanks to Henry Mayer, Sylvia Cleveland, Len Solo, Luther Seabrook, Ida and Studs Terkel, Jo Tackeff, Lee Daniels, Bernice Miller, Charles Hampden-Turner, Edward Carpenter, Phillip Brenner, Larry Olds, Harry Rosenthal, Eugene Callender, Howard and Rosalind Zinn, Andrew S. Young, Ruick Rolland, Armando Martinez, Mel King, Anita Moses, Michael Rossman, John Howard Griffin, H. Jack Geiger, James R. Michael, Ben Scott, Judy Thompson, David Chavolla, Harvey Pressman, Michelle and Larry Cole, Rhody McCoy, Herbert Gans, Carol Chomsky, Duane Dale, Norman Zalkind, Susan Holman and Margot Priest. Thanks, as always in these six years, to my friends and co-workers, Bessie Washington, Joyce Johnson, Yvonne Ruelas, Julia Walker, Margaret Fortes, Ella Wornum, Betty Terry, Eloise Barros, Dotty Chisholm, Joan Whitten, Margaret Putnam, and Mary Lee Warren. Thanks beyond words to my long-time friend, trusted adviser, fellow writer, Annette Holman.

Thanks to you, Barbara, my wife, for telling me that it was time to write this, for helping me to follow through and bring it to completion, and for joining me in this, the first small portion of a struggle which will last all of our lives.

CONTENTS

Free Schools

INTRODUCTION: ORIGINS

SIX YEARS AGO, twelve of the mothers and fathers of the children I had known or had been teaching in the Boston Public Schools sat down in a kitchen with me and with my girl friend one night after supper and decided, with us, to begin a little school outside the public system and available for free to kids whose parents had no money. In making that decision, we were very much aware of doing something different and, as we believed, unprecedented in this city and this nation. There were, to our knowledge, no other "Free Schools" of that nature in existence. There was no movement. We had no literature to turn to. We were obliged to turn only to our own feelings and to our own insights for all comfort, all direction and all guidance.

It was late March of 1966 when we first held a meeting to describe our plans to people in the neighborhood. A good deal of uneasiness and even skepticism greeted our announcement of intentions. When one of the parent-leaders, Julia Walker, announced to the assembled crowd that we would open in September with at least the first four grades, one tall and attractive visitor from Harvard raised his hand and, taking the floor, remarked to Mrs. Walker that it would make more sense to begin small, then add on slowly: "Start with just the kindergarten and the first grade. Then add on another grade each year. Get into the whole thing slowly. It makes more sense to do it that way."

Mrs. Walker replied to him, very simply: "My child is in the fourth grade. That makes more sense."

One of the other academic people in the audience asked how we planned to raise the money to support this hypothetical adventure. He said it in a tone of voice that seemed to question our perception of reality. A member of the parent body rose and answered: "We are going to charge five dollars to everybody who comes over here to Roxbury to listen to our meetings."

So the school had raised its first two hundred dollars.

The next few months were a period of unforgettable energy and locomotion. Sometimes it seemed we gave up eating and sleeping during those amazing days of April, May and June. Parent committees formed and made decisions on specific matters of procedure. A lawyer was found to draw up corporation papers. Parents went home and sat up late at night writing out a set of statements on the kinds of things that they would like to see in a new school. We worked all the separate pieces of writing into one consistent body of short-term intentions and of long-term goals, and we typed it up and had it duplicated. It became our manifesto.

As summer came, teachers were sought out, interviewed and hired. The parents were determined to establish the school upon a viable and non-romantic basis. They offered the teachers significant salaries, competitive with the salaries offered in the public system. They had no money, so perhaps it was not difficult to make exuberant offers. It was all incredible to us anyway.

Having hired teachers, the parents looked for a Headmistress and found her in a striking, thoroughly experienced and politically sophisticated black woman from Chicago. This woman, Bernice Miller, was also offered a competitive salary: something in the order of twelve thousand dollars. It seemed like a great deal of money, but the parents had already hired the teachers and they did not yet have more than the postage money. I guess they thought: Why not go on and hire a Headmistress too?

Next, they had to go and find a building for the school. In speaking of this, parents and kids had often said that they would like to find a building that would not look to anyone like a school: "It ought to look just like a real nice place to go." One day, one of the parents, driving down a street in the midst of Roxbury, stopped her car and saw the building. It was a little red-brick house, with gabled roofs and little diamond windows, and one hundred years of ivy covering it over like an old, old man who never had had a shave or haircut.

It turned out the building was for sale, but the asking price was forty thousand dollars. To me, that seemed an awful lot of money, but we had already hired teachers and a Headmistress and we didn't yet have the first five hundred dollars. I guess we thought: Well, why not just go on and buy a building too? It was a time when many of us felt confident about ourselves and we were not scared to stick our necks out and to take some chances.

In order to buy the building we had to find a bank to help us with the mortgage. The famous old banks of Boston spend a lot of money advertising their good will toward people of all races and religions, but when it comes time to help a group of poor black people buy a building for the education of their children, those idealistic values disappear quite fast. We had to get one-half of the mortgage money from a man outside the city who made us pay him 18 percent interest. I remember that second mortgage very well because I was one of the seven people who put their names down on the line in case the money was not paid. I had to drive out to an isolated ESSO station on a highway south of Boston one night very late, just prior to the stroke of midnight, in order to meet that man in time to sign the mortgage papers. I remember looking down on the paper, as I signed my name against the hood of his white Ford, and wondering how on earth I could back up a twenty-thousand-dollar mortgage with the eighty-five dollars that I then had in the bank. Nobody who signed that mortgage had more than a couple of hundred dollars. I guess that we were lucky to have raised the money: we could not have seemed a very solid business risk, even from the rather special viewpoint of a loan shark.

The next morning, I went up to look at the new building. It was a wonderful old house and after some of the ivy had been shaved away it looked still better. It turned out, after all, that we were not bad businessmen. The building was discovered to be a very fine Georgian period-piece and was appraised, about a year later, for almost eighty thousand dollars.

In any case, we had our own school building. During the weeks that followed, parents interviewed dozens of children, bought supplies, cleaned out the building, hunted for typewriters, tables, desks and chairs. In the second week of September, six months after the original meeting, the New School For Children opened up for its first year. Surprisingly, begun and operated under black control, the school rapidly became a magnet for white families and soon had a waiting list on children who lived far outside the city.

During the subsequent winter, the parents went to the foundations and out into the suburbs and into the churches and into the synagogues and they came back with fifty thousand dollars. In the two years following, the school was able to raise about a quarter of a million dollars. During the same period, two other Free Schools established roots in Roxbury and a fourth experimental venture, called the Learning Center, opened in the South End. Simultaneously, in New York City and in Chicago and in Washington, D.C., a number of other experimental Free Schools very similar to ours began to operate outside the public systems. Within three years of our original church-meeting, we were able to count as many as three dozen ventures of this kind between the Eastern seaboard and Chicago and St. Louis. Within another year, the movement had spread out into the white communities as well; suddenly we became aware of dozens of Free Schools starting up in California. Friends in Seattle told us of an independent schooling-venture planned for something like five thousand children. People called us from Milwaukee to describe the founding of a Federation of Community Schools, comprising seven separate schools that parents had begun to operate outside the system. From St. Paul and Minneapolis and Winston-Salem and Santa Fe and Santa Barbara, from Toronto and Philadelphia and San Francisco and Cincinnati and St. Louis, came letters and phone calls, then newsletters, private papers, Free School magazines and all varieties of confident and hopeful dialogue and interchange. Some of these schools, of course, had started up as early as we, and one or two (as we now learned) had started up before us; but suddenly now, all in a rush around the winter of 1969 and spring of 1970, each of us began to be aware of one another. We started to sense that we were not out on our own, but that we were in fact part of a growing movement.

It was at this point that we began to stop and pause and ask ourselves where we were heading, what we intended, to what kinds of dreams we were accountable and by what values and with what aspirations we were setting forward. It is the purpose of this book to address these questions.

FREE SCHOOL AS A TERM MEANING TOO MANY DIFFERENT THINGS: WHAT OTHER PEOPLE MEAN: WHAT I MEAN: WHAT I DO NOT MEAN

THE TERM FREE SCHOOL is used very often, in a cheerful but unthinking way, to mean entirely different kinds of things and to define the dreams and yearnings of entirely disparate and even antagonistic individuals and groups. It is honest, then, to say, right from the start, that I am speaking mainly of one type of Free School and that many of the ventures which go under the name of Free School will not be likely to find much of their own experience reflected here.

At one end of the spectrum, there is the large, public-school-connected, neighborhood-created and politically controversial operation best exemplified perhaps by I.S. 201, in its initial phase, or later by Ocean Hill–Brownsville in New York. Somewhat smaller, but still involving some of the same factors, and still tied in with the public education apparatus, is the Morgan School in Washington, D.C. At the opposite extreme is a rather familiar type of relatively isolated, politically non-controversial and generally all-white rural Free School. This kind of school is often tied in with a commune or with what is described as an "intentional community," attracts people frequently who, if not rich themselves, have parents who are wealthy, and is often associated with a certain kind of media-promoted counter-culture.

Neither of the two descriptions just preceding would apply directly to the kind of Free School I have tended to be most intensively involved with, though certainly I have been a great deal closer to the first than to the second. There is also a considerable difference in the way I feel about the two. The large, political and public-school-associated ventures like Ocean Hill–Brownsville are, in my opinion, brave, significant and in many ways heroic struggles for survival on the part of those who constitute the most despised and brutalized and properly embittered victims of North American racism and class-exploitation. While these are not the kinds of schools that I am writing about here, they seem to me to be of vast importance and I look upon the people who are active in them with immense respect.

The other end of the spectrum does not seem to me to be especially courageous or heroic. In certain ways, it appears to me to be a dangerous and disheartening phenomenon. I know, of course, that very persuasive arguments can be presented for the idea of escaping from the turmoil and the human desperation of the cities, and for finding a place of physical isolation in the mountains of Vermont or in the hills of Southern California. Like many people here in Boston and New York, I have often felt the urge to run away, especially when I see a picture or read something in a magazine about these pastoral and isolated Free Schools in their gentle and attractive settings of hillside, farmland and warm country-meadow. When I am the most weary, the inclination to escape is almost overwhelming.

Despite this inclination, which I feel so often, I believe we have an obligation to stay here and fight these battles and work out these problems in the cities where there is the greatest need and where, moreover, we cannot so easily be led into a mood of falsified euphoria. If a man should feel, as many people do, that whites should not be working in black neighborhoods, then there are plenty of poor-white neighborhoods in major cities, or neighborhoods of the marginal lower-middle-class along the edges of the major cities, in which we might establish roots and settle down to try to build our Free Schools and to develop those communities of struggle which so frequently grow up around them. I know it is very appealing and, for people who are weary from a long, long period of fruitless struggle and rebellion, it is almost irresistible to get away from everything. I don't believe, however, that we should give in to this yearning, even if it is very appealing and even if we are very, very weary. In any case, I am addressing this book primarily to those who do not plan to run away.

There is one point about the exodus to the woods and hills which is, to me, particularly disturbing. Some of the most conscientious and reflective of the people in the country Free Schools will seek to justify their manner of escape by pointing out that they, and their young children with them, have in a sense "retired" from the North American system as a whole, and especially from its agencies of devastation, power and oppression. Though earnestly presented, this argument does not seem honest. Whether they like it or not, or whether they wish to speak of it or not, the beautiful children of the rich and powerful within this nation are going to be condemned to wield that power also. This power, which will be theirs if they are cognizant of it and even if they aren't, will be the power to affect the lives of millions of poor men and women in this nation, to do so often in the gravest ways, often indeed to grant or to deny life to these people. It will be the power, as well, to influence the lives of several hundred million people who are now subject to North American domination in far-distant lands. Even in the idealistic ritual of formal abdication of that power, as for example, by going out into the isolated hills of Western Massachusetts or into the mountains of Vermont to start a Free School, they will still be profiting from the consequences of that power and from the direct profits and extractions of a structure of oppression.

Free Schools, then, cannot with sanity, with candor or with truth, endeavor to exist within a moral vacuum. However far the journey and however many turnpike tolls we pay, however high the spruce or pine that grow around the sunny meadows in which we live and dream and seek to educate our children, it is still one nation. It is not one thing in Lebanon, New Hampshire, one thing in the heart of Harlem. No more is it one thing in Roxbury or Watts, one thing in Williamsburg or Sausalito, California. The passive, tranquil and protected lives white people lead depend on strongly armed police, well-demarcated ghettos. While children starve and others walk the city streets in fear on Monday afternoon, the privileged young people in the Free Schools of Vermont shuttle their handlooms back and forth and speak of love and of "organic processes." They do "their thing." Their thing is sun and good food and fresh water and good doctors and delightful, old and battered eighteenth-century houses, and a box of baby turtles; somebody else's thing may be starvation, broken glass, unheated rooms and rats inside the bed with newborn children. The beautiful children do not *wish* cold rooms or broken glass, starvation, rats or fear for anybody; nor will they stake their lives, or put their bodies on the line, or interrupt one hour of the sunlit morning, or sacrifice one moment of the golden afternoon, to take a hand in altering the unjust terms of a society in which these things are possible.

I know that I will antagonize many people by the tenor of these statements; yet I believe them deeply and cannot keep faith with the people I respect, and who show loyalty to me, if I put forward a piece of writing of this kind and do not say these things. In my belief, an isolated upper-class rural Free School for the children of the white and rich within a land like the United States and in a time of torment such as 1972, is a great deal too much like a sandbox for the children of the SS Guards at Auschwitz. If today in our history books, or in our common conversation, we were to hear of a network of exquisite, idealistic little country-schools operated with a large degree of personal freedom, but within the bounds of ideological isolation, in the beautiful sloping woodlands outside of Munich and Berlin in 1939 or 1940, and if we were to read or to be told that those who ran these schools were operating by all innovative methods and enlightened notions and that they had above their desks or on their walls large poster-photographs of people like Maria Montessori and Tolstoi and Gandhi, and that they somehow kept beyond the notice of the Nazi government and of the military and of the police and SS Guards, but kept right on somehow throughout the war with no experience of rage or need for intervention in the lives of those defined by the German press and media as less than human, but kept right on with waterplay and innovative games while smoke rose over Dachau . . . I think that we would look upon those people now as some very fine and terrifying breed of alienated human beings.

It is not a handsome or a comfortable parallel; yet, in my judgment it is not entirely different from the situation of

a number of the country communes and the rural Free
Schools that we now see in some sections of this nation. At
best, in my belief, these schools are obviating pain and ether-
izing evil; at worst, they constitute a registered escape-valve
for political rebellion. Least conscionable is when the people
who are laboring and living in these schools describe themselves as revolutionaries. If this is revolution, then the men
who have elected Richard Nixon do not have a lot to fear.
They would do well in fact to subsidize these schools and
to covertly channel resources to their benefactors and sup-
porters, for they are an ideal drain on activism and the perfect way to sidetrack ethical men from dangerous behavior.

SIZE AND RELATIONSHIP TO
PUBLIC SCHOOLS

THE DIRECT OPPOSITE of the all-white rural Free Schools may logically appear to be the large, political, public-school-affiliated venture such as I.S. 201 or Ocean Hill–Brownsville. These schools, for certain, have been two of the most important prototypes of strong and serious urban struggle in the Eastern section of the nation in the past ten years. They also are two centers — or "complexes" — in which some of the most productive work has taken place in the creation and the evolution of a deep sense of black consciousness, of neighborhood participation and of neighborhood control. It is, above all, in the reconstruction of the metaphor and symbolism of the *school itself* as something other than a walled and formidable bunker of archaic data and depersonalized people in the midst of living truth — it is, above all, in the labor of creative repossession of the "marketplace" by its own clientele — that many of us now view ourselves as the direct inheritors of men like Preston Wilcox and Charles Wilson.

There are, however, a number of important reasons for which I feel the need to draw a clear and definite line of demarcation between large ventures of this shape and character and those within which I have tried to take my place and to invest my energies. It seems—to begin with—more than obvious by now that in such areas as New York, Washington, Cleveland, Boston or St. Louis there cannot be much serious role for white men and white women in the genesis of these operations. They constitute, in almost every situation, an important portion of the black and Spanish process of self-liberation and of self-determination. Their function is as much political as pedagogic. They are enormously significant in community organization. They are not, however, a sound or reasonable context for active and conspicuous participation on the part of white men.

There is a second reason why I have not chosen to participate in — or write about — these large, political "subsystems." The kinds of public-school-affiliated operations I now have in mind, no matter how inventive or how passionate or how immediately provocative, constitute nonetheless a basic extension of the ideology of public school. They cannot, for reasons of immediate operation, finance and survival, raise serious doubts about the indoctrinational and custodial function of the public education apparatus. No matter how sophisticated or how inventive these "alternatives within the system" may contrive to be, they nonetheless must continue to provide, within a single package: custodial functions, indoctrinational functions, credentializing, labeling and grading services, along with more purely educational functions such as skill-training. The public-school-affiliated ventures such as those that I have named above, or such as Parkway School in Philadelphia or Morgan School in Washington, D.C., may constantly run skirmishes on the edges of the functions and priorities of domestication; in the long run, however, they cannot undermine them. The school that flies the flag is, in the long run, no matter what the handsome community leader in the startling Afro likes to say, *accountable to that flag* and to the power and to the values which it represents. This is, and must remain, the ultimate hang-up of all ventures which aspire to constitute, in one way or another, a radical alternative "within the system."

There is a third reason, also, why I am not involved with public-school-associated ventures. This reason has to do with size. It has been my experience that something bad happens often to good people when they go into programs that involve large numbers of young people and a correspondingly extended political constituency. The most gentle and least manipulative of people often prove to be intolerable "operators" once they are faced with something like two thousand children and four thousand angry parents. Even those people who care the most about the personal well-being of young children turn easily into political performers once they are confronted with the possibilities for political machination that are created by a venture that involves so many people and so much publicity. There are those, I think, who have been able to resist it to a large degree. Kenneth Haskins is one of several important leaders in the Washington and New York area who seem to have been able to maintain a comfortable balance between politics and education in the face of formidable odds. The point, however, is that those odds are *there* — and they are very much against us.

Then, too, and possibly the most important, the likelihood of going through deep transformations and significant alterations of our own original ideas (by this I mean the possibilities for growth and for upheaval in our consciousness of what "school" is about) is seriously circumscribed when we become accountable to fifteen city blocks and to ten thousand human beings. This is perhaps a somewhat impractical position. I just think many more remarkable things can happen to good people if they happen in small places and in a multiple of good ways. Even a school of five hundred children and two thousand parents, friends and teachers, hangers-on and teacher-aides, seems much too large. The Free Schools that seem to have the greatest chance of real success, not just in terms of publishable statistics, but in deep human terms as well, are those in which there are not more than eighty to one hundred children.

It may be I am only justifying my own inclinations. I know that I feel far more comfortable and can be in better touch with my own instincts and with my own sense of justice in a Free School that remains as small, non-formidable and non-spectacular as possible. When I first read Paul Goodman's essay about "mini-schools," I felt it sounded coy and unrealistic. Today I believe that Goodman is correct in arguing for a limited size and for a modest scale of operations. It is not easy in this nation to resist the emphasis on bigness, growth, constant expansion. It is, however, something well worth fighting to resist, if it is in our power to do so.

I am, then, speaking for the most part about Free Schools (1) outside the public education apparatus, (2) outside the white man's counter-culture, (3) inside the cities, (4) in direct contact with the needs and urgencies of those among the poor, the black, the dispossessed, who have been the most clearly victimized by public education, (5) as small, "decentralized" and "localized" as we can manage, (6) as little publicized as possible. It is time now to go on to the first essential point of business.

POWER: PARTICIPATION: SANCTION:
LEGAL MATTERS

FREE SCHOOLS, in order to be able to receive tax-free donations, have got to "incorporate" themselves in square, old-
fashioned legal terms. In mechanical respects, the setting
up of a nonprofit corporation is a simple matter with a competent lawyer. I have seen an attorney set up the whole thing
in just about two hours. Moreover, in most cities, Free
Schools shouldn't have to pay for this. If the American Civil
Liberties Union lawyers will not help, and frequently they
won't, there generally are a number of well-known movement lawyers who will do the job for free. This part, therefore, is routine.

What is not routine — and what, in my experience,
has proven to be a very complicated and risk-laden area of
choice and tactics — is the difficult decision as to what specific kind of Trustee Board or governing structure the group
in question wishes to create. Many people who go into Free
Schools are so nervous about power, and so uneasy in regard
to anyone who holds it, that they do not like to face the painful fact that somebody in this school, or at least some group
of bodies, is going to have to make some kinds of difficult decisions. To people who have never been through this, what
I have just said may seem self-evident. It is an unhappy

truth, however, in many Free Schools I have known, that
nobody wants to believe that power is a real thing, that it is so
real that it exists even among ten people, that it cannot be
ignored and that those who pretend to ignore it end up speaking of it, dealing with it and suffering for it more than anybody else. The composition of the Trustee Board, and the
power that it will or will not have, is therefore elemental to
the entire character and oftentimes to the survival of the
Free School.

Several Free Schools which were first created and origin-
ally conceived by a small group of men and women have
immediately inflated both their numbers and importance by
creation of a large, "significant" Trustee Board. It is as if
they feel no sense, or very little sense, of self-awarded sanction for the things that they may do, and feel — almost like
children — that they need to find some other people who are,
somehow, more "significant" than they to give their school
a sense of authenticity or strength. Many of us feel so little of
self-authenticated "license for creation" in our own hearts,
by the time we finish school, that we are afraid to try for
anything important unless we have first gotten "permission"
from somebody else who seems more powerful and more
important and already "authorized."

The consequence of this is, in some cases, that the school
creates a large, important and prestigious Trustee Board
which does, indeed, have plenty of muscle in its dealings with
the system, but is inherently artificial in its make-up since the
members do not share the same ideas, or even a little patch
of common ground. Free Schools that set out in this way have
been able sometimes to survive, but not without internal
decimation and unhappiness which have left permanent
scars.

My own belief is that either the Trustee Board should be so fluidly and so openly defined as to be virtually identical with the total parent, teacher and student population of the school, or else that it should be very small, composed only of a few intensely close and trusting friends, and function henceforth as a benign dictator. In other words, there should either be a total commitment to full democratic participation of all people in the school or else there should be a straightforward, small and honest "power-structure." Either method seems to work well, just so long as those who come into the Free School recognize and understand this is the way it works. What does not work well is something halfway in between: a large, political, multi-faceted Trustee Board, generally representing ten or twenty different interests, cliques, or subgroups, and constituting, in effect, a nonstop, left-of-center version of the Oxford Union in which two dozen people regularly contend for power, glory, grandeur, reputation. These kinds of competitive and often vitriolic governing institutions have murderous consequences. Those who choose structures of this kind may well have good and sober reasons for the choice they make. They ought to know, well in advance, however, that most of the Free Schools which have set up large and complicated governing structures of this kind have not been happy and have not been strong.

Some of the decisions as to the kind of Trustee set-up that a school establishes will, of course, be determined by the motives that inspire the Free School in the first place. There are some Free Schools that announce their intention to function at the will and by the decision of the pupils they enroll. This kind of school cannot, without inherent contradiction, attempt to lock up legal power in a small Trustee Board. If the school says, for example, and if it really means, that it is to be the vehicle of the wishes of the children and teen-agers and of whoever else may wish to come on deck, then it is dishonest to retain the power in a few hands. In such a case, there might be a "revolving" Board, elected by all people who desire to vote, or possibly just by those who actively participate, or only by those who are studying and teaching in the school. There is also the ultimate and, in certain ways, the ideal set-up of a Free School with no Trustee Board at all, but just a paper corporation to live up to the regulations of the law. In many ways this is the most appealing plan because it cancels out the contradictory image of a group of radical people duplicating, even in their Free School, the same symbolic structures they have wanted to escape. It also cuts down on the idea of "someone else above us" which is always present even when there is a Board of Trustees that does not intend to exercise much power. I know of at least three Free Schools that have managed to function in this way. It is also possible for schools to begin under one set-up and transform themselves gradually into the other. Whatever is done, the most important thing is to avoid a situation in which power becomes a "prize" and where the competition to possess it becomes more important than the happiness or the survival of the children.

The least democratic, least hip and least participatory arrangement — i.e., a small, benevolent dictatorship — is, to be quite blunt, a remarkably good and reasonable way to govern a small school. If the school, for example, consists in effect of four or five energetic parents, three or four teachers and a spin-off group of twenty or thirty additional parents, friends and teachers who are acquainted with the others, it seems both legitimate and proper for the eight or ten people who comprise the "core" to incorporate themselves as the legal trustees of their own creation, and to live henceforward with the odium, if that is what it is, of being known to others as a group of people who intend to keep hold of their own dream.

It is possible that I would not have made this statement six years back. It is, however, a statement which grows out of six years' sharing in, and watching others share in, minor conflicts of the most extraordinary sort across the tables of School Meetings, School Boards, Boards of Trustees and the like. In five cities, and in dozens of widely separated cases, I have never yet seen a situation of this kind where the consequent disputation did not demean and undermine the character of those who were involved and where it did not also plant the seeds of future decimation. There are, in addition, a number of well-documented situations in which a school, begun by open, unsuspicious, politically trusting, idealistic people, was simply and plainly taken over by a skillful group that knew the way to pack an open voting-session and, immediately after, went about the work of turning the school into an image of its own conception.

There may be certain situations in which the dialectic struggle of opposing power-blocs, the all-night meetings, the weekend "retreat" for sensitivity sessions and the rest are reasonable and valid. I do not think, for example, that it would be damaging, or at least not intolerably so, to have this competitive process taking place within an institution that involves exclusively adult affairs and does not tamper with the lives of children. Even with children involved, it might not hurt so much to have this kind of contestation taking place within a rural context of well-set and physically unthreatened human beings. In a case like that of a Free School in the midst of an embattled city, where survival is often a desperate business and where something very much like siege conditions frequently obtains, I think it is important to be careful that we do not use the children for the sake of our own egotistic joy in being able to boast to one another of our "wide-open" and "participatory" nature. I tend to be turned off by people and by groups that advertise this kind of claim. Too often, what one finds is that they have superbly "open" and wholly "participatory" sessions, often lasting well past one or two o'clock at night, "relate" beautifully, "communicate" honestly, "touch," "feel" and "open up" to one another marvelously, but never seem to arrive at the decisions that their children's lives and the survival of their school depend upon, grow totally exhausted and end up closing in six months. It seems to me that people who are looking for group therapy ought to find it somewhere else and not attempt to work out their own hang-ups at the price of eighty children.

The preceding words, of course, stand in some conflict with the current fashions. I am trying, however, to be realistic, unromantic and as candid as I can. There is a time when we must sit down and compose rhapsodic stories to raise money for the Free Schools. There is another time when we have got to try to be as honest as we can. In 1972, the Free Schools have come into their own hour. It is the time for candor.

BUILDINGS: HEALTH CODE: WAYS TO NAVIGATE THE LABYRINTH

EVERY TIME I meet with a group of Free School people to discuss the problems that each one of us has faced, sooner or later somebody makes the point that getting hold of a suitable building is often the most difficult part of the whole thing. Incredible Building Codes, obtuse bureaucracies and openly inconsistent supervisors seem to be a number of the constants in the ritual of North American oppression. The Building Code, so blatantly and often tragically ignored in cases of old, collapsing, rat-infested tenement houses owned by landlords who have friends within the city's legal apparatus, are viciously and selectively enforced to try to keep the Free School people out of business. Nothing else, in my own experience, including the rottenness of the people who control the Boston Public Schools, has radicalized my own ideas and attitudes so much as the behavior of the Fire Department, Building Department and the Department of Public Safety of this city and this state. It is the same in many other sections of the country. The same red tape, the same pretended innocence as to our political affiliations, the same attempt to base oppressive and discriminatory judgments on objective grounds. If municipal agencies wanted to set out to devise a strategy for turning gentle and utopian liberals into cynical and rage-

minded radicals, they could not do a better job than by im-
posing upon the Free Schools both the out-of-date regulations in themselves and the out-of-date human beings who
come in to enforce them.

It is, to start with, very difficult for Free Schools in the
Northern cities to go out and purchase their own buildings.
The New School did this, and some others have done it also;
most of the time, it proves financially impossible. Banks do
not like to give mortgages either to blacks, to young
people, to people who are young *and* black, or to people
who are working in black neighborhoods. The most familiar
strategy, then, is either to rent a building or else to try
to get part of another organization's building at low cost or,
possibly, for free. This is the point at which you start to run
into the business about Building Codes.

In Boston, it is easier to start a whorehouse, a liquor store,
a pornography shop or a bookie joint than it is to start a little
place to work with children. The regulations are detailed
and complex: you need to have front and rear exits, halls
and stairways of a particular width, walls and ceilings (in this
city, anyway) of wire-lath construction, as well as a certain
number of acceptable toilets, washbowls and the rest, depending on the number of young people who will be involved. If the program is going to involve really little children, it generally has to take place on the ground floor.

In themselves, these kinds of rules seem to make sense.
Nobody wants to work within a building that is dangerous
for children. It is, however, the capricious way in which these
regulations are enforced that gives us so much trouble.
Many of the regulations, for example, have extraneous details and wholly gratuitous amendments which function
somewhat like those fifteen-mile speed limits in small towns

on Cape Cod. The rock-jawed officer sits there quietly in his car and watches folks he knows go by all day at thirty-five or forty, but when he sees a kid with long hair or a black man who does not appear to him to fit the style of a Cape Cod summer visitor of the proper kind, off goes the siren with the blue light spinning and pretty soon he's pulled you over to demand your license and to ask if you can't read or just don't give a damn about the law. The Building Code in Boston is exactly like that. If it were enforced consistently, a significant number of the best-known landlords turned philanthropist and friend to politicians, judges and the like would land in prison.

The set-up is so transparently unjust in Boston that Elijah Adlow, the Chief Justice of the Municipal Court, repeatedly continues or throws out the charges of code violation brought against the most powerful and most hated landlord in the city, refuses to apply or exercise the five-hundred-dollar daily penalty and fine which exists precisely in order to put teeth into the Building Code, refuses to deliver bench-warrants for this man's arrest when he and his lawyer fail to show up in the courtroom, yet does not hesitate either to deliver sermons to young people on the need for law and order, or to deliver lectures to the residents of ghetto neighborhoods on their proper obligations as slum tenants.

Last year in Boston, one of the buildings owned by the rich man in question — a man named Maurice Gordon — went up in flames and burned to death eight of its tenants. Fire Department and Building Department records later indicated that the building had been visited and examined approximately one year before the fire, but that no action had been taken on its multiple violations. The Building Commissioner explained that he had at length given up hope of seeing effective action taken against this landlord and the other major landlords because the cases he had brought in previous years had been repeatedly continued or thrown out by the Chief Justice and by other judges. He had been, at once, psychologically and legally conditioned to know where — and in the face of whom — the law should either be enforced or disregarded.

As I write, I have in my hand a flier given to me three days ago by the little boy across the street. It is an announcement from the Highland Park Free School: "The Building Inspectors will not certify our building . . . The Building Commissioner will not give us a building permit . . . Spread the word . . . Our school is in danger of being closed down." Today they went to court. The five-hundred-dollar daily fine has now been threatened to intimidate them into closing down. The prospects for the winter are not cheerful. Last year the powers of the law closed down another of the parent-operated Free Schools for three months on the same pretext. "My school is closed," the boy across the street said to me earlier today. He has just had his first imperishable lesson in the nature of equal justice before law.

To some it may appear that matters of this sort do not have a place within a book about the strategies of Free Schools. To my own way of thinking, these are the most important matters; for they give the whole sense of the character of struggle and the context of injustice and gross exploitation that we work within. It is of far more importance that we have to fight against the likes of the Chief Justice and his friends than it is that we use tri-wall to make chairs and tables or that some teachers may prefer the "Batteries and Bulbs" of E.D.C. to someone else's science unit. I am, frankly, much more interested in the community of conscience that a Free School at its best can constitute, and in the consciousness of struggle that it is able to create, than in the multi-faceted details of our choice of science games or math equipment. In the back section of this book, I list a number of good sources to supply the answers to the detailed needs and questions which pertain to science, math and other areas of subject-matter. Several writers, including George Dennison and John Holt, have offered hundreds of concrete, valuable suggestions of this kind. My goal in writing this small handbook is not to repeat the work that they have done, but to bring some portion of my own life and my own experience into the Free School dialogue.

Whatever the obstacles and the harassments we may face, there are at least a couple of strategic possibilities that I have seen or heard of in the struggle to obtain a suitable location. First, it is a fact that cities tend to waive a number of restrictions for church buildings or for church-related structures such as parish-houses. Even when they don't, the churches are most often built in ways that meet a number of the most important regulations. It is also true, unfortunately or not, that many of the older churches and the church-related schools in poor black neighborhoods now are starting to go out of business. This is especially the case in cities such as Boston and Milwaukee that have formerly had large numbers of parochial schools but where the Catholic population has been moving out. The same is true, of course, not just for Catholic churches and church schools but for the Jewish synagogues and Hebrew schools as well. A lot of buildings therefore have already been approved in earlier times for pre-school, church school and for public gatherings. Unless these structures are in total disrepair, municipal agencies will not often run the risk of being charged with obvious and provable discrimination by suddenly determining the buildings to be unacceptable. Moreover, the congregations that are moving out will often be prepared to help a group of people who are setting forth on something like a school or pre-school, which appears at least to be so much of a benign and innocent endeavor.

It is perhaps a little disconcerting in its symbolism to think of our children studying and learning in the worn-out shell of someone else's church or parish-house. It is a little like a symbol of the neighborhood itself, which is most often a hand-me-down from previous generations of poor people. Still, if the building is good and if the fact of prior ownership by church or synagogue can help to get you past the Building Code, it may be worth the symbolism. Symbols have a way of disappearing if the new life in the old shell is exuberant and vital and conveys its own symbolic power.

The other logical channel that I know, which has been used in Boston and New York, is to get hold of a building in the midst of a section which is slated for mass demolition — but not yet — and which, in the meantime, has been taken over by the city. Urban renewal, here in Boston as in most other Northern cities, does not often work to the advantage of poor people. In the midst of the process of expropriating poor slum tenants to build new high-rise structures for the middle-class and upper-income people, there is, however, one unexpected dividend for a Free School. A lot of times, the government agencies in question will assign a block or a number of blocks to major demolition for a long-range program of construction, evict the companies that have a factory or storage warehouse or commercial property of any kind, but leave the tenants in apartments for a time. If the interval at stake is only a few months, it isn't of much use; but it often happens here, as in New York and Philadelphia and some other cities, that the interval between removal of commercial properties and demolition of the actual structures will be five years.

The urban renewal organizations may, of course, refuse to help us. In many cases, though, they are so much on the defensive and so bitterly disliked, as the direct result of their unpopular actions, that they will be willing to cooperate with a small and innocent-appearing Free School, for whatever the dividend in neighborhood affection it may win them. I know of one group that was given use of a warehouse structure for four years at only forty dollars' rent a month; two others, each of which got a block-wide supermarket. It is not much fun to have to go through all of the red tape and all of the petty obstacles that municipal agencies and private corporations seem to set up in our path. It is, on the other hand, at least one way of finding out what kinds of cities and what kinds of economic obstacles poor people are obliged to live with and confront. Like many of the other things that we must do when we are starting out, it is a tedious and exhausting business that proves only later on to have been worth the struggle.

HARD SKILLS: READING: BAD JARGON
AND UNEXAMINED SLOGANS

MORE FREE SCHOOLS go to pieces over the question of the "teaching of hard skills" — and the teaching of reading, in particular — than over any other issue that I know. I would like to try, within this section, to say what I have come to believe in this regard. In the back pages of this book I will give leads for those who may, in differing degrees, support or take exception to my views. In my own experience, within the cities and in the suburbs, too, there are often as many as ten or fifteen children out of twenty-five or thirty who learn to read in much the same way that they learn to tell time, navigate the streets of their own neighborhood or talk and play games with each other. It seems self-evident that for these children a rigid and regular process of repetitive instruction, such as any formal reading method generally entails, is just a total waste of time and only tends to mechanize and to devitalize the child's sense of words as symbols of his own life and of his own imagination and creative powers. I say this so that the rest of what I say will not be misconstrued.

The rest is this: For an awful lot of children, for as many as one-quarter or one-half of the children in a Free School situation, it is both possible and necessary to go about the teaching of reading in a highly conscious, purposeful and sequential manner. This is the kind of square and "rigorous" statement that you do not often hear within the Free Schools. It is, however, the sort of thing that needs very much to be emphasized right now, because there has been too much uncritical adherence in this movement to the unexamined notion that *you can't teach anything.* It is just not true that the best teacher is the grown-up who most successfully pretends that he knows nothing. It is not true, either, that the best answer to the blustering windbag teacher of the old-time public school is the Free School teacher who attempts to turn himself into the human version of an inductive fan.

To keep the record clear, and in order that my own views will not be misunderstood, I believe today as strongly as I did eight years ago in 1964 that all education should be "child-centered," "open-structured," "individualized" and "unoppressive." It is on this basis that we carried out our struggles for reform within the Boston Public Schools. It is also on this basis that we set out to begin our own schools. There is no question now of turning back to a more circumspect position. There *is* a question, however, about the ways in which some of the people who first come into the context of the Free Schools often seek to *force* their new-found orthodoxies in between the teeth and down the throats of black and Spanish-speaking children and their mothers and their fathers. Many of the young white people who come into Free Schools straight from college are incredibly dogmatic and, ironically, "manipulative" in their determination to *coerce* the parents of poor children to accept their notions about non-coercive education. In Thomas Powers' book about Bill Ayers and Diana Oughton, there are some interesting passages on this subject. Ayers was the founder and one of the central figures in one of the original Free Schools in this country: a school that he started in Ann Arbor, Michigan, in 1966. The school went to pieces for a number of reasons but, most of all, according to Powers, on the old issue of the teaching of hard skills. "The single most important failing of the school, and the one on which it foundered in the end," as Powers writes, "was the fact that no one learned to read there." Ayers believed, according to the standard jargon, that the children would "ask" someone to teach them to read as soon as they "really wanted" to read. In the three years of the school's life, Powers says, "that time never seemed to arrive." In another passage, Powers makes the observation that the life of the school ended on a bitter note, partly because of the official harassment which had plagued the school but, more important, because of rejection by the blacks. Ayers and his friends were committed to helping the black children, but "rejected the terms on which the black parents wanted their children to be helped." Later on, people would tend to blame the school's collapse on the harassment of public officials. In fact, however, the school failed because parents were taking out their children.

I admire Bill Ayers, and I am not writing this in order to hold him up to criticism. The point is that the process here, in all its details, seems to me a classic sequence. White men and women who come in to teach and work alongside black and Spanish people in the kinds of small, committed and exciting Free Schools that I have in mind, have got to exercise their ideologies and their ideals in dramatically different ways depending on the situation they are in and to perceive these differences with great sophistication. It is a bitter pill for many young white people to accept, but in a large number of cases those rewards and skills and areas of expertise which many of us consider rotten and corrupt and hopelessly contaminated remain attractive and, in certain situations, irresistible to poor people. It is, moreover, often a case not of material greed but of material survival. There's not a lot a poor young kid fourteen years old can do in cities like New York or Boston if he cannot read and write enough to use the telephone directory or to understand a telegram or to read a street sign. It is, too often, the rich white kids who speak three languages with native fluency, at the price of sixteen years of high-cost, rigorous and sequential education, who are the most determined that poor kids should make clay vases, weave Indian headbands, play with Polaroid cameras, climb over geodesic domes.

It is not necessary, in speaking about reading, to adhere to either of two irresponsible positions. It is as much an error to say that learning is never the consequence of conscious teaching as it is to imagine that it always is. The second error belongs most often to the public schools: the first to many of the Free Schools. The truth of the matter is that you *can* teach reading. Lots of people *do*. I have taught children to read on a number of occasions, and I have done this in situations where they very likely would not have learned to read for several years if I had not assumed a clear initiative. George Dennison has done the same. So too have the teachers and the parents of the Highland Park Free School. So too have the people at the Southern School out in Chicago. It is true, as I have said above, that it is frequently not necessary. Where it is not necessary, it is obviously ill-advised. Where it *is* necessary, but where in the name of Joy and Freedom it is not undertaken, then I believe the mothers and fathers have very good reason for their anger.

Many of those children who enter the Free Schools after a number of years already spent in public school come to identify the printed word with so many painful and intimidating memories that they are, in a sense, shell-shocked and numb in any situation that has to do with books and with black ink. The consequence of this, especially if it should be the situation of a child who is already ten or twelve or, as in cases that I know, fourteen years old, is a complete avoidance of all contact, all possibilities and all inclinations in the direction of a piece of written matter. The child is often almost literally "frozen" in regard to reading. If he is ingenious and sophisticated, as many of the fourteen-year-old street kids in the South End are, he may be able to disguise his fear of words to a degree that will successfully deceive the young white teachers. "He's beautiful," as the young utopian volunteers will characteristically remark. "He just likes cinema and weaving more than books. When he's ready for books . . . when he senses his own organic need . . . he'll let us know."

The horrible part of this is that the volunteers in question really mean this and, moreover, often believe it with a dedication which denies all possibility for self-correction. I have seen this happen sometimes four or five years in a row. Children can get messed up very badly by that foolish and insistent obviation of the simple truth that they are in real trouble. It is too much like looking into the windows of a mental hospital and making maniacal observations on the beautiful silence of the catatonic patients. Children who are psychologically shell-shocked in regard to reading are not "beautiful" and are not in the midst of some exquisite process of "organic" growth. They are often in real trouble; they are, in the most simple and honest terms, kids who just can't do a damn thing in the kinds of cities that we live in. There must be a million unusual, non-manipulative but highly conscious ways of going about the task of freeing children from this kind of misery. There is only one thing that is unpardonable. This is to sit and smile in some sort of cloud of mystical, wide-eyed, non-directive and inscrutable meditation — and do nothing.

In the back section of this book there are a number of specific references on reading. Many good ideas are offered in *The Lives of Children*, by George Dennison. In the now familiar and, by now, somewhat dated books of Sylvia Ashton-Warner there are several ideas that I have found successful. James Herndon and Herbert Kohl both make a number of specific recommendations about reading. I have had the most success with a combination of approaches: in one case even making profitable use of a square, sequential, rather rigorous, old-fashioned phonics method, but tying it in with a lot of intense and good discussions about the struggles and the needs and longings that the kids in question lived with in their homes and in their neighborhoods. From these discussions came many of the words that seemed to the children to be most highly charged with intellectual voltage or with a kind of sensual exhilaration. Certainly words like "sex" and "cops" and "cash" and "speed" and "Eldorado" are likely to awaken the interest of the fourteen-year-old children that I know a good deal quicker than "postman" and "grandmother" and "briefcase." I also find that many children who think they cannot read and must begin from zero are excited to find that "GTO," "GM," "GE" or even "CBS-TV" are, at the same time, words *and* letters which they already understand quite well: indeed so well they do not think they have the right to call this reading.

Some of these ideas are elaborated in much greater depth, and within the context of a logical sequence and consistent pedagogic framework, in the very important books and essays by the Brazilian scholar, Paolo Freire. It is difficult to summarize Freire's position and his practice in a single sentence or in a single phrase. The heart of his approach, however, has to do with the recognition and identification — on the part of the learner — of a body of words which are associated with the most intense and potentially explosive needs and yearnings in his own existence. Freire speaks of these as "generative" words: first, because they generate the thirst, the love, the passion, the motivation of the learner; second, because out of these words — out of their syllables and phonic units — new words can then be generated. It is not clear to me or my co-workers that Freire's views can be applied in direct fashion to our situation here in Boston or New York; for one thing, much of his approach is tied to methods of syllabication that are workable in Portuguese and Spanish, less so in English. The ideological and pedagogic basis of his method is, however, brilliantly adaptable and is ideally suited to our situation and our struggle.

Freire's writings are listed in the back pages of this book. They are, to me, among the most intelligent and inspired writings that I know within the field of education and of reading in particular. His methods are, of course, inherently political in their character. I do not believe that they can be applied without immediate repercussions in the public school. They are, however, ideal materials for discussion and for possible application in the Free Schools.

HARD SKILLS IN GENERAL:
WHITE ANGUISH: BLACK DESPAIR

THE ISSUE OF READING opens up the larger question of the purposes and function of a Free School in the context of a black or Spanish, economically cheated and politically disenfranchised neighborhood. Inevitably, by reason of birth and education and associations built up over years of life and shared experience, I am often in closer contact with some of the young white teachers than with certain of the older and more moderate black parents. I nonetheless believe very strongly that it is unwise and generally not to the advantage of poor children to have the items and particulars of the white man's counter-culture foisted upon them by their teachers. It is especially destructive if this is attempted to the direct neglect of certain obvious survival matters.

Many of the young newcomers to the Free Schools refuse to recognize the very considerable degree to which their own risk-taking attitudes and "anti-system," "anti-skill," "anti-credential" confidence is based upon the deep-down knowledge that in a single hour they could put on shoes and cut their hair, fish out an old but still familiar piece of plastic from their pocketbook or wallet, go to Brattle Street or go to Bonwit Teller, buy new clothes and walk into a brand-new job. Some of us do not like to let on that we have, in fact,

this sense of intellectual and financial back-up. The parents
of poor children, however, recognize this sort of thing quite
clearly. They also recognize, with equal clarity, (a) that
their own children do not have protection of this kind,
(b) that, without a certain degree of skillful and aggressive
adaptation to the real conditions of the system they are
fighting, they will simply not survive, (c) that much of the
substance of the white-oriented counter-culture is not of real
assistance in that struggle and in that adaptation.

Visiting and talking twice with Ivan Illich and his col-
league Everett Reimer during the course of seminars in
Cuernavaca, I have twice come back to Boston to confront
the hard realities that still must shape decision-making here.
It is very appealing, at two thousand miles' distance, to
entertain the notion of an educational experience that does
not involve credentials or curriculum or an interlock of
hard sequential labors. In immediate terms, in Boston and
New York, it is in my opinion both unwise and perhaps
destructive to attempt to close our eyes to the existence of
such matters. It is, rather, essential, I believe, to face up to
the truth that these credentials and these measured areas of
expertise and certified abilities comprise, as of now, the irreducible framework for our work and struggle.

In speaking of this issue I find myself in the difficult position of one who respects Everett Reimer and who admires
Ivan Illich but who also lives in Boston in the year of 1972.
I try to find the meeting-place between these widely separated
points of reference in something which I often speak about as
"waging guerrilla warfare with credentials." I would like to
join in court suits, as co-witness or co-litigant or co-plaintiff,
in order to challenge and confront the present racist, stupid
and pernicious character of College Board examinations

I would like to join in campaigns of obstructive, meddle-some and — wherever necessary — illegal civil disobedience in the offices of the men who govern and control the Educational Testing Service. I would like to join in the campaign of words initiated by John Holt and Ivan Illich and which addresses itself to the question of illegal job discrimination on grounds not just of race, religion, sex or years, but also on grounds of previous years of "certified domestication and indoctrination" in the public schools. I would, moreover, like to go beyond the war of words and take specific actions to provoke some deeper public recognition of the unjust character of this credential-apparatus as it now exists. Numbers placed upon our foreheads at the present time are evidence less of competence achieved than of the impotence with which we have been willing to proceed along uninterrupted avenues of self-debilitation. I think that we should force these issues on the public consciousness by every means at our disposal.

There are, moreover, a number of less public but no less important means of carrying out the campaign of guerrilla actions that I have in mind. The most dramatic way by which to emphasize the insubstantial character of the present twelve-year interlock of public education is to develop methods by which to short-circuit these sequential and curricular obligations. Twelve years of lockstep labor in the field of math or language arts are manifestly wasteful of a child's learning energies and learning hours. Freire teaches basic literacy in forty days. No child who is not brain-injured or otherwise impeded in his powers of comprehension needs six years to learn to write ten sentences with reasonable cogency and power. The three-year French or Spanish language-block required by most high schools and by certain of the college-entrance stipulations can usually be transcended in three months by methods such as those used both by Illich and by the U.S. State Department. Various portions of the high school math curriculum can be abbreviated and condensed in somewhat the same fashion. Several Free Schools now are carrying out exciting and inventive methods of short-circuit of this nature. This is, however, a very different thing from acting as if the system of credentials, once ignored, will fall to pieces. The citadel does not need to be revered or loved in order to be stormed and conquered. It is insanity, however, to behave as if it were not there.

The anguish and concern in this regard that many of the parents of poor children feel and often bitterly express, when faced with white men and white women who appear to scorn such non-ecstatic matters, cannot of course be seriously comprehended if we do not vividly perceive the real-life needs and desperations and injustices with which poor people in this nation and in this decade still must co-exist. The sharp taste of social insult, hunger, sickness, physical alarm, the siren's scream and the blue light spinning in the neon sky, the desperation of young mothers in the back-street clinic of a miserable Northern city-slum: these are the metaphors of truth and pain which still must shape our judgments and decisions. In my neighborhood, one family of three children and their mother, who have been my friends now for six years, lives on an annual income of three thousand dollars. Another family, to which I have been drawn through friendships with two of the oldest children, has survived some twelve-month periods in the past few years on eighteen hundred dollars. There are ten children in this family. Men and women who are locked into such lives as these cannot be expected to look without uneasiness or even without considerable alarm at those who tell them that their children do not need degrees, do not need math or English, do not need to find out how to psyche out an exam, do not need college, do not need money, do not need ugly, contaminated, wicked, vulgar, middle-class "success." The issue for the children that I have in mind is not success. It is survival.

The lives of children in the immediate neighborhood in which I live constitute, by any index and by all criteria that any reasonable man might have in mind, medical, economic and educational disaster areas. Black children in this neighborhood with basic competence the same as that of any child in the midst of North Dakota or in the wheat fields of Nebraska are, statistically, by fifth-grade level, at least one year behind their white suburban counterparts in basic coding and de-coding skills like math and reading; by seventh-grade level, two years behind; by ninth-grade level, three years; by twelfth-grade level (if they ever get there) four or five years. Statistics for the Puerto Rican children in this neighborhood of Boston are, if possible, still worse than those for blacks. Ninety percent of the Puerto Rican kids in public school in Boston drop out of school before they get into the tenth grade. In a Puerto Rican population of approximately forty thousand people, there are at this writing less than seventy children in *all levels* of the public high schools. The odds these children face, first on surviving the attrition-rate between first grade and twelfth grade, then on being able to go on to higher education, are approximately one-twentieth the odds of kids in ordinary white suburban schools, one-thirtieth the odds of kids in places such as Evanston and Greenwich, one-fiftieth the odds of kids who go to places like St. Paul's and Exeter and Groton.

The medical odds with which the children in these neigh-

borhoods must live are even more alarming. Black children
in the United States have approximately twice the chance of
dying in the first twelve months of life as white children
born in the same section of the nation on the same day. The
national average is twenty infant-deaths per thousand. In
white suburban neighborhoods, the figure is much closer
to fifteen. In black communities like Harlem, Watts and
Newark, the figure seldom runs lower than thirty or thirty-
five and, in some areas, it runs as high as fifty. It is commonly
assumed that the most serious instances of catastrophic
health-conditions, of deficient diet and of inadequate medical
service are to be found within the rural South. In the event
that we feel smug, however, in our Northern point of view,
Dr. H. Jack Geiger of Tufts–New England Medical Center
points out that there are a number of Northern ghetto census-
tracts in the United States in which the infant-mortality rate
exceeds *one hundred deaths* for every thousand children.
This figure transcends the curse visited by the Hebrew God
upon the land of Egypt in the Book of Exodus, wherein it
was decreed that every tenth child born to an Egyptian
woman should be born dead.

It is desperately important, in my own belief, that those
of us who join together to create and nourish a community of
conscience in the concrete substance of a small and passionate and dedicated Free School should understand, deep in
our heart and soul, before we start, the grave, immoderate
and inescapable dimensions of the human context of our
struggles and our labors. For poor people in the United
States the risk of dying prior to age thirty-five is four times
the average for the nation as a whole. In certain areas of
the Deep South, the death-rate for black women in the act of
giving birth is now six times the rate for whites. Ten to

fifteen thousand people, mainly black and Puerto Rican, die
an unnecessary death each year in New York City: statistically, they fall into the category called "excess mortality."
The figure for newborn infants nationwide is estimated to
be as high as forty thousand. The heaviest concentrations of
these infant-deaths are in the rural slums of the Deep South
and in the Northern ghetto. These forty thousand children
are the victims of gross medical injustice, both created and
maintained by the surrounding white and middle-class population which derives direct and measurable advantage from
the unjust allocation of available resources. There is no way
to classify these children other than as the victims of social,
professional and institutional murder.

Those children who survive the hour of their imperfect
birth incur a number of equally formidable dangers in the
first few years of life. The medical consequences of lead
poison from the lead paint used in much of Boston's worst
slum housing are now gradually coming to the attention of
the parents and community leaders in these neighborhoods.
The crumbling plaster is covered with sweet-tasting chips of
lead paint that poor children eat or chew as it flakes off the
walls. The lead paint poisons the brain-cells of young
children. Infants die, are paralyzed, undergo convulsions and
sometimes grow blind, if they chew it over a long period of
time. The forces of the law in Boston do not compel a landlord to replace, repair or cover over the sweet-tasting crust of
paint that paralyzes children. The law *does* allow a landlord
to take action to evict a family if the mother or father misses
one rent-payment by as much as fifteen days. Even in those
cases where the technicalities of the law might ordinarily be
to the advantage of the black man or of the black woman who
is the tenant of the house in question, it is repeatedly proven

to be the case that judges in this city, as in most others in the North with which I am familiar, will not seriously penalize nor publicly embarrass those rich and powerful owners of slum properties who are their friends, the friends of politicians who appoint them or, as in some instances that we have seen in Boston in the past two years, the major contributors to political campaigns.

It is in this context, then, that sane and sober parents of poor children in such cities as my own draw back in hesitation, fear or anger at the often condescending if, in the long run, idealistic statements and intentions of those who attempt to tell them to forget about English syntax and the preparation for the Mathematics College Boards but send away for bean seeds and for organic food supplies and get into "group-talk" and "Encounter." It seems to me that the parents are less backward and more realistic than some of their white co-workers are prepared to recognize. It seems to me that a tough, aggressive, skeptical and inventive "skill" like beating out a tough and racist and immensely difficult examination for the civil service, for City College or for Harvard Law School, rings a good deal more of deep-down revolution than the handlooms and the science gadgets and the gerbil-cages that have come, in just five years, to constitute an Innovative Orthodoxy on a scale no less totalitarian than the old Scott Foresman reader.

To plant a bean seed in a cut-down milk container and to call this "revolution" is to degrade and undermine the value of one of the sacred words. To show a poor black kid in East St. Louis or in Winston-Salem or in Chicago how to make end runs around the white man's college-entrance scores — while never believing that those scores are more than evil digits written on the sky — to do this, in my scale of values, is the starting-point of an authentic revolution. It is not to imitate a confrontation, but to engage in one. It is not to speak of doing "our own thing," but rather to do one thing that really matters and can make a visible difference in the lives of our own brothers in the streets that stand about our school. Harlem does not need a new generation of radical basket-weavers. It does need radical, strong, subversive, steadfast, skeptical, rage-minded and power-wielding obstetricians, pediatricians, lab technicians, defense attorneys, Building Code examiners, brain surgeons. Leather and wheat germ may appear to constitute a revolution in the confines of a far-removed and well-protected farm or isolated commune ten miles east of Santa Barbara or sixteen miles south of Santa Fe; but it does not do much good on Blue Hill Avenue in Boston on a Sunday evening if a man's pocket is empty and his child has a fever and the buses have stopped running.

There has to be a way to find pragmatic competence, internal strength and ethical passion all in the same process. This is the only kind of revolution that can possibly transform the lives of people in the land in which we live and in the time in which we are now living.

PERMANENT STRUGGLE: LOCATION:
LIFE-STYLE: CONFRONTATION

FREE SCHOOLS cannot function as life-giving and impassioned organizations if they do not have the means or will to generate a brilliant, strong and self-renewing sense of permanent struggle. Many Free Schools that I know in Boston, and in some other areas such as New York City, begun in a state of mind which is white-hot, intense, determined and inexorably involved with human struggle, derive from this their deepest energies, their deepest consciousness and their most solemn sense of good comradeship. Much of this consciousness, in my belief, comes from the sense of direct confrontation with the public schools, as well as from the kinds of confrontations with municipal offices, Building Code, the First Inspector and the rest, that constitute a large part of the early struggle to establish the new venture. In particular, though, it is the sharp and recent memory of public school: the knowledge, vivid, strong and constantly renourished, of just how brutal, trivial and life-taking public school within a ghetto neighborhood can be. It does not require an incantation of the Summerhillian Gospel, neither does it ask the reading of Important Books on "serious social issues," to remind the mother of a six-year-old black child in the South End of this city to look into her child's eyes at four o'clock when he comes home from school and see the fire and the bitterness burning there.

Then, too, the visits that a worried mother makes to the principal's office at the local public school, the defensive statistics and the falsified sense of amicable good will in the deceitful eyes of principal or guidance counselor or schoolteacher, the stale air and the hypocritical symbols, pledge of flag and words of anthem, photograph of Lincoln, King or Frederick Douglass on the classroom wall — the whole thing burns into the mind and stirs the life-desiring coals of pain and rage within the desperate consciousness of those who must repeatedly experience its bitterness.

If, to this sense of recent insult, insurrectionary anger and sharp pain is added the exhilaration of the opening months and hours of a new and promising experience in the conception and then in the concrete, growing realization of the Free School, a fine, pure pitch of burning energy and of remarkable and unexpected confidence develops. It is the kind of time in which we grow and learn, and feel astonished at our capability to keep on going with so little rest or sleep. We live on doughnuts, glasses of milk or hurried "potluck suppers" in the midst of wonderful, insane and crazy nights of money-raising tactics, strategies, campaigns, decide at midnight to put out a spectacular mailing the next morning, type up the stencils, ink over the millions of dumb errors that we make, dig up the minister-friend of someone else's minister-friend who said it was okay to use the ditto-machine in someone else's Unitarian Church or someone's storefront office, break into the office, run off the stencils, do it ten times badly, finally get it almost right, breathe in the wonderful stink of the mimeograph ether, pile the new copies, staple, fold and label, find the misspelled headline just too late, argue and laugh, get out a bottle of cheap wine, drink from paper cups, go home and sleep four hours, wake up feeling terrific and then start all over.

"The exuberance of crisis," a group of my friends wrote when they were in the early stages of a kind of Free School venture of their own in Pennsylvania, "highlights the poverty of our daily experience . . . The assertion of communal solidarity makes us feel more keenly the personal frustration of our normal routine. The expression of outrage against immediate evil bears the emotional intensity of all the anger unspoken each day, carries our entire burden of sadness and bitterness. The taste of revolution, the breath of promise it brings to our troubled lives, confirms the sense of desperation which we daily face."

Paolo Freire has written that one of the most familiar consequences of the "culture of silence," not only in the Third World but also in the internal colonies of the United States, is the loss of "subject status" in the consciousness of human beings, and in its place a sense of being always consequences ("objects") of the processes and the historical events initiated and conceived by others. If this is an accurate perception of our situation, then the kind of dynamic experience that I have just described is perhaps a classic example of the process of expropriation by the poor man of his own purloined and alienated sense of moral leverage. The saddening part, however, is the quite remarkable speed with which almost any process of creation and regeneration can become banal and routinized within this nation at the present time and, in this case, the quite astonishing speed with which a group of parents, children and their teachers can give up or somehow lose, even without the knowledge of the loss, that sense of passion and vocation that first burned within them.

The question, then, in my own sense of struggle, is as follows: How can the Free School achieve, at one and the same time, a sane, on-going, down-to-earth, skill-oriented, sequential, credentializing and credentialized curricular experience directly geared in to the real survival needs of colonized children in a competitive and technological society; and simultaneously evolve, maintain, nourish and revivify the "un-credentialized," "un-authorized," "un-sanctioned," "non-curricular" consciousness of pain, rage, love and revolution which first infused their school with truth and magic, exhilaration and comradeship. Few schools up to now seem to have been able to do both; some that I know, however, come extremely close.

It is hard, I think, not to transform ourselves in six months or one year from a bold and eloquent brotherhood of strength, street-logic, liberation, into a bunch of OEO-assisted, *New York Times*–admired, Model Cities–favored, Carnegie Foundation–visited "program administrators," "innovative educators," "resource people," "para-professionals" and all the rest. The very language used in the preceding phrases suggests the rapid degeneration of the Free School vision into a world of dull, un-brilliant, mediocre jargonese: "delivery of services," "secondary impact," "replicable features," "individualized curricula," "open-structured processes," "urban-oriented resource areas . . ." If, on the one hand, the hang-loose hippie dialect represents a jargon of centrifugal release from sanity and honest and unarguable need, the bureaucratic jargonese reveals the still more devastating trap of Instantaneous Domestication. There has got to be a way to be "free" without being maniacally and insipidly euphoric, and to be consistent, strong, effective, but not tight-assed, businesslike and bureaucratic. Either direction represents a falling-off from our original and authentic vision. The true, moral, political and semantic derivation of "Free School" lies in "Freedom School." It is to the liberation, to the vision and to the potency of the oppressed that any Free School worth its derivation and its photographs of Neill, Tolstoi or Eldridge Cleaver must, in the long run, be accountable. If we lose this, in my judgment, we lose everything.

Several immediate tactical considerations seem to me to be a part of the above discussion: I think, first of all, that a great deal rests on physical location. The ideal location for a Free School born of the frustrations and the discontents of ten years' struggle to transform or liberate the public school is not across the city but *across the street* from that old, hated, but still-standing and still-murderous construction. I know that such an appropriate and explicit sense of physical confrontation is not always possible; nor, of course, does the visible reminder of the miserable and monolithic enemy assure the radical integrity or the revolutionary perseverance of the Free School on the opposite corner. It is, perhaps, a little easier and more sensible to state it in the opposite terms. A Free School which, by accident or intent, ends up in the most expensive, marginal and physically respectable section of a total neighborhood in torment is certainly a great deal more likely to lose sight of its own reason for existence than the school which, like the New School in its first three years in Boston, is straight across the street from that old haunted house that flies the U.S. flag, or which, like Harlem Prep, is in a renovated supermarket straight on Eighth Avenue in Harlem. The farther the distance from the place of pain, the less the reason to remember the oppressor's eyes or to be cognizant of his abiding powers.

It is hard, indeed, to worry about, or even really to believe

in, the existence of lead-paint-poisoned infants or of vindictive, steel-eyed cops, while strolling in the anesthetic gardens
and the foliage-decorated courtyard of the Ford Foundation,
still less in the privileged pavilions of somebody's all-white,
upper-class Free School in the sloping mountains of Vermont
or amid the red rocks and the perfect sunsets of Fort
Collins, Colorado. The Free School that stands foursquare
on the scene of struggle, in such physical, hard and graphic
fashion as I have just proposed, cannot within the course of
ordinary days fail to be stirred, provoked, inspired and at
times enraged by concrete processes which take the form of
real-life visions in the windowpane. Strong parents in the
public school across the street begin to organize. They want
to know if we will let them use our school for their initial
planning-sessions . . . Six of the younger and less domesti-
cated teachers in the nearby junior high ask us if they could
bring their kids into our "Black Action Workshop" after
regular school hours . . . They also ask us if we would support their presence at the School Committee Hearings on the
following Wednesday night . . . Two months later, three
hundred kids and fourteen teachers from the same school
stage a "walk-out." Their walk-out turns into a "walk-in,"
into the parent-operated Free School on the nearby corner
. . . Together we plan a picket line for Friday . . . They
hold "their" press conference in "our" kindergarten . . .
Our kindergarten kids unplug the TV cables . . . interrupt
the questions . . . humanize and give five minutes of excited, partisan and unexpected exhilaration to the press re-
porters who suddenly see, in the realization of our dream,
what it is that those within the low-security prison on the
opposite corner are protesting . . .

This is the kind of high-stake and high-voltage substance

and experience that make for permanent struggle and strong
loyalties. In Roxbury, Massachusetts, on Leyland Street, a
beautiful Free School, nourished and sustained by eloquent
young parents and good teachers, discovers that several of
its children are in grave medical danger as a consequence of
lead poison in the peeling paint and crumbling plaster of
the nearby tenement houses. They canvass the neighborhood, enlist physicians, fire broadsides at the press . . . Forty
children in the neighborhood turn out to have been poi-
soned by the lead paint . . . The school itself becomes the
scene of medical examinations for all children, not just
those who are the members of its student body . . . The
liberal press does one or two brief stories . . . The courts
do little . . . the city agencies still less . . . In the winter,
a child in Roxbury dies of lead-paint poison . . .

The Free School is in the midst of true and human confrontation with the real world of exploitation and oppression that the law, the rental patterns and the medical profes-
sion constitute. Teachers at the school do not need to send
away to Westinghouse or E.D.C. for "relevant" social studies
units "oriented to some of the more serious issues in the
urban situation." Most public schools, and a large number
of the Free Schools too, nourish an atmosphere which is de-
void of almost all true, credible experience and in which
only arduous simulations of real processes take place. The
ultimate paradox to which such gruesome institutions finally
arrive is the introduction of that paradigm vehicle of school-
delineated alienation: "the simulation game." We close up
the windows, pull down the blinds, ventilate the air, deflect
the light, absorb the sound, etherize the heart and neutralize
the soul; and then we bring in "simulation games" to try to
imitate the world we have, with such great care and at such

consummate expense, excluded. The twelve-million-dollar stone-and-concrete junior high school without walls and also without windows stands at the corner of the two most turbulent and most explosive streets within the "inner core." Inside, the "innovative," "open-structured" "teacher-as-a-resource-person" introduces to her locked-in class of black and militant, cheated and embittered eighth-grade children a "simulation game" called GHETTO: "Let's pretend now that we live within one of the racially impacted regions of the Northeast section of the country . . ."

Alienation can seldom have reached a more exquisite pitch than this.

The sadness, though, is that the Free School can with consummate ease develop the same ironical situation of the mirror created to reflect the real thing that we dare not look at. The reason, I suppose, that we fall into this state of mind so easily is just that so many of us, or almost all of us, have been "well-schooled." As such, we think of school, even of Free School, in almost all of the same terms that we lived by when we were ourselves "schoolteachers" or "schoolchildren." The simulation-ritual is the perfect metaphor of public education in its present form. The Free School that can break this mold of artifacted process receives the almost instantaneous reward not only in a heightened sense of loyalty and strength in its adult ranks but also in the sense of strong and unmanipulated motivation on the part of its own children. It doesn't take a lot of bullshit speeches about the need of a neighborhood for good black doctors, lab technicians, chemists, biologists, biochemical analysts and such, when the little boy across the street dies of the lead paint on the walls of his own bedroom.

"Relevance" and "urban-oriented" are the twin-curricular

code phrases in this nation, at the present time, for the ritual-experience of looking into the mirror at the battle being waged behind our back while walking rapidly away from it. The Free School that shatters the mirror and turns to face the flames is the one that will not lose its consciousness of struggle or its capability for a continual process of regeneration. When we forget the enemy's name, we turn our guns upon each other. The guerrilla martyrs who lost their lives within the mountains of Bolivia understood this very, very well. Morale declined, paranoia thrived, internal decimation soared, when the periods of time between significant confrontations grew too many and too long-extended. Free School parents in Boston and New York begin to turn their guns on one another, and on their chosen teachers and their own Headmaster and Headmistress too, only when they forget the power and calculation of a man like Albert Shanker or the personal brutalism of a woman like Louise Day Hicks. The location of the Free School, the vivid and repeated confrontations in which it is willing to engage with the immediate manifestations of municipal exploitation on all sides, the degree to which it identifies its own survival with the struggle of those across the street who still are locked within the public prisons — these are the kinds of things that seem a great deal more important than the number of stamped and sanctioned "Innovative Methods" that we bring into our little space of liberation, learning and regeneration.

In his book, *The Storefront*, Ned O'Gorman writes these words:

A fire inspector comes to bug us about a minor violation . . . I take him out onto the sidewalk and shout out loud to the people there, and to the people looking out of windows that finally someone has come to inspect their houses and do something about their suffering . . . The inspector knows and I know that he has come to bug the storefront . . . In the guise of inspectors the city suddenly appears to check up on restaurants, schools, shops, day-care centers, and playgrounds. Yet families can suffer an entire winter without heat or hot water and no inspector ever appears to challenge the landlord.

This passage, brief and offhand as it seems, says a great deal of what I have been trying to express about the sense of consciousness, of permanent struggle and of immediate, unmanipulated, honest activism within the context of a Free School. There is much within O'Gorman's book that I do not agree with; in this regard, however, I am in complete accord with his whole impulse and with his instinctive way of getting mad. It seems to me of great importance that we do not forget how to get very, very mad, and at which people.

TEACHERS WHO ARE NOT AFRAID
TO TEACH

FREE SCHOOL, as the opposite of public school, implies not one thing but ten million different possibilities. Those who intend to build one strong and honest structure of their own creation, no matter how imperfect or how unenlightened in the view of those who have read different books or come from different places, have got to be prepared to be not only clear but also sometimes merciless, sometimes obsessive even, in the lucid and inexorable repetition of the values and the purposes by which they live and labor: "This is what we are like, and this is the kind of place that we are going to create. This is the kind of thing we mean by freedom, and this is the sort of thing we have in mind by words like teach and learn. This is the sort of thing we mean by competence, effectiveness, survival. If you like it, join us. If you don't, go someplace else and start a good school of your own."

Precision and directness of this kind seem obvious and simple. They are, however, frequently the rarest of commodities within the Free Schools. Many of the Free School people have been far too frightened of the accusation of being headstrong, tough, authoritarian, and by direct result have tried too hard to be all things to all potential friends and allies. There is an additional reason, also, for our hesitation to speak out in clear self-definition. It is the fact of loneliness and of uneasiness within the possible crossfire of a hostile and oppressive social structure. It is especially difficult to scrutinize or to resist the offered willingness to be of help at times when we are most acutely conscious of this loneliness and isolation.

The issue comes into a sudden focus in the choice of teachers, as well as in the choice and in the substance of curriculum. Free Schools which exist within the siege conditions of New York or Boston, or one of the other Northern cities, do not need to be ashamed to offer and provide a strong, substantial, down-to-earth classroom experience in which the teacher does not hesitate to take a clear and visible position as a knowledgeable adult. This is not to advocate political indoctrination of young children. It is, however, to concur in the opinion of large numbers of black leaders that young children in these situations need strong models in effective, bold, risk-taking, conscientious and consistent adults. It is for this reason that I find myself in frequent opposition to much of the calculated indirection which appears to be one characteristic of the counter-culture.

There is a certain degree of paradox within the clash of needs and interests which are represented here. The young white woman or young white man, fresh from years of very expensive education and intensive intellectual preparation, endeavors to laugh away his real credentials and to conceal or to deny the inescapable power and authoritarian truth of his unquestioned competence. The colonized, manacled, trapped and often broken black man yearns for competence, dreams at night of recognizable credentials and would give his heart and soul to know the feel of an authoritarian effectiveness in the face of crooked cops and paid-off judges. I believe, for this reason, in the kind of Free School in which power, leverage and at least a certain degree of real sequential labor are not viewed with automatic condescension or disdain. I believe in a school, as well, in which effective adults do not try to seem less powerful than, in reality, they are. I believe in a school, therefore, in which the teacher does not strive to simulate the status or condition either of an accidental resource-person, tangential consciousness, wandering mystic or movable reading-lab, but comes right out, in full view of the children, with all of the richness, humor, desperation, rage, self-contradiction, strength and pathos which he would reveal, as well, to other grown-ups.

There is a way in which some of us lock ourselves into a foolish and untenable position in regard to the real power which we do possess and in regard to the deep convictions which we hold. There is a destructive and intolerable form of classroom power based upon manipulative behavior and the arbitrary function of position. This we condemn in public school and properly condemn within the Free School also. There is, on the other hand, the obvious and inevitable power of the man or woman who is — in simple words — much better skilled, more widely informed, less circumscribed in recognition of the options, better defended against the presence of deceptions, less innocent of illusions and more cognizant of possibilities than plump little six-year-olds in yellow trousers and red jerseys. It is familiar, among large numbers of the adults in the rural Free Schools, to pretend to abdicate the very significant and important power which they do possess and do continually exercise upon the lives of children, most significantly, of course, by placing them, to begin with, in this artificial context of contrived euphoria within a world in pain: a context within which they can neither hear the cries nor see the faces of those whose oppression, hunger, desolation constitute the direct economic groundwork for their options.

Pretenses of this kind are just not honest if, in fact, the adult does exert the deep, continuing and unquestioned power of the man, or of the woman, who has first planned and then conceived and executed this whole context in the first place. Some of the Free Schools that describe and advertise their all-white high-priced innovative education in the pages of *New Schools Exchange* seem often to build the core of their life-style around the simulation of essential impotence: with competence admitted only in those areas of basic handiwork and back-to-nature skill in which there is no serious competition from the outside world inasmuch as there is neither function, use nor application in the social interlock in which we are obliged to live. "Wow!" I hear some of these Free School people say. "We made an Iroquois canoe out of an oak log!" Nobody, however, needs an Iroquois canoe. Even Iroquois do not. The Iroquois can buy aluminum canoes if they should really need them. They don't, however. What they need are doctors, lawyers, teachers, organizers, labor leaders. The obvious simulation-character of the construction of an Iroquois canoe by a group of well-set North American children and adults in 1972 is only one vivid and easily identifiable portion of the total exercise of false removal from the scene of struggle which now typifies the counter-culture. There may be some pedagogic value or some therapeutic function in this form of simulation for the heart-sick or disoriented son or grandson of a rich man. It does not, however, correspond to my idea of struggle and survival in the context of the streets and cities that I know.

In the face of many intelligent and respected statements,

writings, essays on the subject of "spontaneous" and "ecstatic" education, it is simple truth that you do not learn calculus, biochemistry, physics, Latin grammar, mathematical logic, constitutional law, brain surgery or hydraulic engineering in the same spontaneous and organic fashion that you learn to walk and talk and breathe and make love. Hours and seasons, months and years of long, involved and — let use be quite honest — sometimes non-utopian labor in the acquisition of a single unit of complex and intricate attainment go into the expertise that makes for power in this nation. The poor and black, the beaten and despised, cannot survive the technological nightmare of the next ten years if they do not have this kind of expertise in their own ranks.

Nothing could be more terrifying evidence of the gulf of race and class that separates oppressor and oppressed within this nation at the present time than that so many of those people who are rich and strong beyond all precedent, beyond all previous human expectations and beliefs, should toil with all their heart and soul to simulate the low-key hesitation and the calculated stammer and awkward indirection of an artificial impotence, while blacks in Roxbury, in Harlem and in East St. Louis must labor with all their soul to win one-tenth the *real effectiveness* which those white people so deliciously and so luxuriously conspire to deny. If there is a need for some men and some women to continue in that manner of existence and in that frame of mind, and if it is a need which cannot be transcended, then let there be two very different kinds of Free Schools for a time, and let there be two very different kinds of human transformation and of human struggle; but let us, at least, within the Free Schools that we build, and work within and labor to sustain, let us be willing to say who we are, and what we think, and where we stand, and what we strive for, and let us also say what things *we do not want.*

There is one portion of the total syndrome of pretended impotence which is most dangerous and most subversive of the long-range struggle for survival in an urban Free School. This is the manner of operation which Bernice Miller often speaks of as an inclination toward The Insufficient — or what I think of sometimes as The Cult of Incompletion. It is the kind of hang-loose state of mind which looks with scorn upon the need for strong, consistent and uninterrupted processes of work and aspiration, but makes a virtue rather of the interrupted venture, of the unsuccessful campaign. I have in mind an almost classic picture of a group of rural Free School people that I know, sitting on the lawn of someone's country-farm or "radical estate," in a mood, almost too comfortable, of "resting on our elbows at a place of satisfying retrospect on our own failure" or at a kind of "interesting plateau of our half-success." There is, at times, almost a sigh, as in the fresh-washed air after a rain: "We did not win and are not burdened with the future. Instead, we can externalize our failure, blame the system, blame the Carnegie Foundation and reflect, perhaps with a lot of eloquence and with a lot of sensitive insight, on the comfortable vista of a lost campaign." Eloquent Failure, in such instances, becomes the Free School's version of success. It must be obvious that this is murder in a Free School for poor children.

I think that it is time for us to face this problem of our own inherent fear of strength and of effectiveness head-on. I think that we must be prepared to strive with all our hearts to be strong teachers, efficacious adults, unintimidated leaders and straightforward and strong-minded provocations in the lives of children. I think that we must work with all our

hearts to overcome the verbal style of debilitation and sub-
junctive supposition: the interposition, for example, of the
preposition or conjunction of arm's-length invalidation
("like") before all statements of intense commitment or
denunciation. There are some Free School leaders and some
Free School writers that I know who now begin to justify and
to defend the will-to-failure by making a virtue of the capability to start and stop things in response to sudden impulse.
The sophisticated Free School is the one that rises and col-
lapses like the sun in its own hour or like the year in its own
season. It is a curious revolution, in my own belief, which
builds its ideology and its morale upon the cheerful prospect
of surrender. Men who walk the city-streets with minds un-
cluttered by their own internal need for self-defeat, eyes open
to the pain and desperation in the lives around them, could
not conceivably make barbarous recommendations of this
kind.

The Free School press and Free School writers speak more
often of Bill Ayers' Free School, up in Ann Arbor, which did
not work out, than they do of Edward Carpenter's remarkable and long-sustained success at Harlem Prep. I have said
in an earlier section that I have a great deal of respect and
admiration for Bill Ayers. Still, it cannot be easily by-passed
or ignored that, insofar as the Free Schools are concerned,
Bill Ayers' experience is perhaps the very prototype of the
Eloquent Exercise in self-defeat. I believe we can and ought
to honor people like Bill Ayers. In the same way, many of
us love and revere the name of Che Guevara. There is also
Fidel, however, who was not afraid to sit within the victor's
chair, and there are also strong and stable people like Ed
Carpenter. It would not hurt us to have upon the walls or
in the stairways of our little schools not only photographs of

those who do not fear to die for their beliefs, but also photographs of those who do not fear to win. I think that the children of the black and poor ought to be able to know, and ought to be able to believe, right from the first, that the struggle for liberation does not need to end with sickness in the mountains or with steel helmets in Chicago or with a T-group in Manhattan. It can also end with personal strength, political passion, psychological leverage and the deepest kind of moral and imaginative power.

I do not intend to mock young people, or myself, or my own friends, who really try and honestly do fail; but I am thinking also of the anguish of success and the related anguish of "too much effectiveness" for those who look upon effectiveness itself as bearing the copyright of evil men. There is no reason why we need to choose between a contaminated sense of competence upon the one hand and a benign sense of ineptitude upon the other. The preference for the unsuccessful, for the interrupted enterprise, for hesitation and for low-key aspiration, is not surprising or inexplicable within a hard and driving nation like our own. It is, however, incredibly destructive and debilitating to the spirit of a Free School. There is all the more reason, then, in the light of dangers of this kind, that we be willing to define ourselves with great precision, with deep reiteration and, if need be, with remorseless candor.

POSTSCRIPT: In terms of sheer logistics, it often proves almost impossible to do what I have just proposed: i.e., to keep on stating and restating where we stand on all the issues that may possibly occur. It is, for this reason, often of great help to do one or a number of the following four things:

1. Write out a very short but clear and definite statement

in regard to *just those detailed areas* within which Free
School disagreements most repetitively occur: reading; curriculum; discipline; teacher-style; survival goals; political
consciousness; or whatever else. Don't say: "We are in favor
of freedom," "We think every child ought to learn at his
own pace," "We think that every child is unique and beautiful." This kind of idiotic jargon means so little, or perhaps
so much, that nothing in the way of clear self-definition is
achieved by its reiteration. Everyone who comes into the
Free School, theoretically, believes that "children should be
free." The real question is what we *mean* by freedom. This
is the part that ought to be spelled out.

2. Make a cartridge tape recording of this statement, or
tape the first or best of several conversations of this kind. Ask
every man or child who comes in to visit as prospective
teacher, parent or as pupil to sit down and listen to the tape
before all else. If it is totally abhorrent to their tastes and
wishes, it may make them angry but it certainly saves a lot
of wasted time.

3. Hire someone who is reasonably good at coping with
all kinds of strangers, visitors, friends or enemies, as they
may turn out to be, and let the job consist above all else in
this one labor of self-definition. It does not sound like a very
satisfying or invigorating job; perhaps, therefore, it can be
attached to something else which is more vital and more fun.
However it is arranged, it seems essential that all those who
come in from the outside to observe or visit or sign up must
be made cognizant of what we do, and who we are, and how
we function, long weeks and hours before there is a chance
for misery and recrimination to set in.

4. Establish, as many of the Free Schools do, a period
of "internship" or of "trial participation" for all adults —

regular teachers, parent-teachers, or teen-age trainees —
and let it be understood well in advance that this is the standard procedure *for all people* who join up and that there is
no special odium or insult in the idea of the trial session.
Ideally, in order to be effective and in order not to cause last-
minute panic, the trial session ought to be set at least two
months or more before the time at which the intern is to start
in on a regular basis: in the summer months, for example,
or, as in some cases that I know, during the last weeks of the
spring semester. In this way, if it does not work out to both
our satisfactions, there is still time both for the intern to find
other jobs and for the Free School to find other interns.

Finally, there is this one important point:

Free Schools in all sections of the nation often prove to be
of almost irresistible attraction to some of the most unhappy
and essentially aggressive people on the face of the wide earth.
Sometimes it seems that God has punished the Free Schools
for attempting to steal fire from the Heavens by making them
into magnets for the most tormented and, at times, vindictive
people. In many instances, the very same people who have
been "evicted," in a sense, from someone else's Free School
somewhere else, precisely for the pain and hurt they cause,
will shop around until they come to us. There is, as many
people in the Free Schools find, a rather familiar kind of man
or woman who does not in fact care a great deal about
children but enjoys a power-struggle almost like a piece of
raw meat. There is a kind of "energy of devastation" in such
people which can be helpful when it is directed outward at
external obstacles, but which can be incredibly destructive
when it turns in on our own small numbers.

I have seen one of the kindest of black people that I know
pause — look gently — almost with sadness — into the eyes

of someone of this sort, and just say in quiet words: "Well, you don't seem to be somebody that I want to work with. There has been too much unhappiness among us since you came. You do not seem to think we are sufficiently enlightened. You do not seem to think that we have read the right books. You may be right. We have not read many books in the past year. We have been too busy trying to build up our school and trying to keep off people who bring sadness and unhappiness into our ranks. We think that you are just that kind of person. Leave us alone to our unenlightened state of being. We would rather have the courage of our errors than the kind of devastation forced upon us by your intellectual wisdom."

I had not wanted to include the preceding passage in this book. It shows too much of the bitterness and the deep, deep pain which have been part and parcel of the Free Schools that I know. It seems, though, that it wouldn't be honest to leave this kind of business out. It breaks the illusion of simplicity and grace encouraged by the kinds of stories published in some of the national magazines. It certainly runs counter to the myth that all the people on the Left are beautiful and healthy. There are surely as many screwed-up people in the Free Schools as in any other left-of-center movement that has taken root within this nation in the past ten years. The thing that is important is that some of the Free Schools have been able to resist or to transcend large numbers of these problems. They do it, for the most part, by remaining small, declaring their own position in political and pedagogic terms with absolute precision and no hesitation, excluding too many visitors, avoiding unsolicited affiliations, steering clear of jargon, staying away from bureaucratic operations, and not being ashamed in any way of their real power, and not attempting to disguise it. I hope that some of the details and some of the suggestions that I have presented in this section will be of practical help to Free Schools which intend to will one thing, and then to stick with that one thing, and see it through to a responsible and visible completion.

DEFINITION OF SURVIVAL

THERE IS A STRANGE and bitter process which we see in operation in this nation at the present time by which a number of
solemn, painful and important words — each of which in
itself has deep and obvious meaning, resonance and conno-
tation — can be "defined" and "neutralized" and "processed" by the cerebral skills of those who write and speak of
social change and social revolution in terms which do not
have a great deal of direct or practical connection with the
things they talk about. The word *survival* is a good example
of the process that I have in mind. It is a word that does
mean something concrete. It does not mean the struggle
to find depth and richness in the soul of life. It does not
mean the struggle to live at peace with surfeit and excess in
Palo Alto. It does not mean being able to go out into the
woods of Northern Michigan and play at being a woodsman
or a farmer for one season and then coming back and telling
people that we have "survived." There is a way, however, in
which a word like this can lose its whole truth and whole
power and can be turned instead into the sort of non-essential
and non-desperation matter which then is appropriated
without remorse, and even with considerable fascination, by
comfortable people who "survive" quite well by any ordi-

nary standards. It becomes something complex and something intellectual. It becomes the "search for value" in the Age of the Machine. It becomes the longing to return to the Good Things of the Old Times. It becomes a ride into the country.

The kids I know in the South End of Boston happen to enjoy — and dream about — a ride into the country as much as any children that I know. The poor people and the black people that I know appreciate and value pleasure, peace, escape from anguish, happiness and love as much as any young white person or as much as any white adult. In spite of the implications of much of the counter-culture literature, rich white people in blue jeans and beads did not all at once discover sunshine, the smell of the warm earth in April or the good taste of homemade bread in winter. It is just that they alone have the inherited freedom and the lobotomized consciousness to build a whole life-style out of the possession and the monopolization of these luxuries, while the men they have empowered, by their abdication, to hold governance in this nation are destroying the wide world with fire and napalm.

In the best of all possible worlds, with no men starving and with no small children hungry and untreated, with no injustice and no mechanized oppression and no direct and racist exploitation of the Third World by the First, it would be fun to speak no longer of words like conflict, struggle, pain and mandate, but only of words like Ecstasy and Joy, to speak not of the character of death for those who lie beneath the hobnails of our shoes but only of the "quality of life" for those who do the marching. We do not live in such a world, however, and it is not merely incorrect, therefore, but brutal, devious or self-deceived, to speak or write as if our greatest difficulties and most important challenges, in school or out, were not direct injustice and the ice-cold capability for anesthetic self-removal from the consciousness of guilt and pain, but rather a somewhat limited supply of delectation or, to state it as a number of educators do, a prevalence of "joylessness."

In the face of myth, in the face of lies, in the face of mass manipulation, in the face of "survival tools" like windmills, potter's wheels and hand pumps advertised within the pages of the *Whole Earth Catalog,* in the face of rugged and exciting camping trips known as "survival training" and marketed in the name of Outward Bound to those rich men and women who are doing fine without it, in the face of all this high-class hokum and deceit, there still is a literal meaning for the word survival. Children that my wife and I see every day go in the streets year after year with raw, untreated sores, swollen wrists, scars on their throat and shoulder from untreated injuries of years before. Men and women that I know, and have known now for several years, go for ten years or fifteen years with huge and ulcerated tumors on their arms and shoulders. I know one child who is now eighteen years years old. She falls down in the middle of the city, at Grove Hall, on Blue Hill Avenue, in Orchard Park. One night she comes downstairs into the coat-room underneath the church-stairs which is the office of a Freedom School. She asks me, please, if I would close the door and hold her head within my arms: she is about to have an epileptic seizure. She says she does not want to interrupt the other children in their classes. I watch her as she undergoes three seizures in a row and, in between, the terror closing in, as in a child's bad dream that you can't get out of. When she can stand, we drive to Boston City Hospital. There is a three-hour wait before she gets to see the intern. He comes out at last and gives her an injection of some tranquilizer to sedate and to relax her. He writes out the prescription for Dilantin and for Phenobarbital. He looks at me then and shakes his head and says to me, one white man to another: "It's a goddamn shame. Nobody needs to have an epileptic seizure in this day and age . . . Nobody except a poor black nigger."

Hundreds of children that we see as students or as neighbors in the streets are born in the Deep South under conditions that are beyond the imagination of most white men. In many instances, the mothers of the children that we know have lived for so long on a diet of rice, fatback and beans, no beef, no butter and no milk, that they cannot adequately nourish their own infants. The children grow up in a state of nonstop desperation. They are born without hospitals, nurtured often without milk, schooled without love, indoctrinated without learning and grow to their tormented manhood without help of dentist, pediatrician, surgeon or eye doctor. The only "equal care" they ever get is in the amicable supervision of the local precinct-captain.

The drug statistics in our neighborhood are beyond almost all calculation. In Boston, the school-age population among black and Spanish children is, at the lowest, forty thousand and, at the highest, fifty thousand human beings. In the age range twelve to eighteen, it can be established at approximately twenty thousand. At least two thousand of this number are users of heroin: one out of ten as a conservative statistic. Heroin addiction exists, of course, out in the suburbs, as well as in the city. The consequences of heroin addiction, however, follow racist lines. In practical terms, in realistic working-out of odds, occurrences, statistics: heroin addicts who are white, Protestant or Jewish, middle-class, suburban, go to the Institute for Living in Hartford, to the McLean Hospital in Waverly, or to a place that nobody else will ever hear about two miles west of Zurich, Switzerland. Heroin addicts who are black or Spanish go to the Industrial School for Boys if they are under eighteen, to the State Reformatory in Concord if they are eighteen or older, or else, approximately one time out of a thousand, and at considerable saving to taxpayers, straight to the graveyard with a well-placed bullet in the back part of the brain.

It is in the context of these kinds of lives, and it is in the daily contact with these kinds of needs, that we must raise the question of the old, original and unsophisticated definition of the word survival. It is frustrating, and disheartening, to me and to my wife that so much of the literature of social change and human transformation depends upon the willingness to forgo short-term, clear and visible mandate in favor of the possibilities of long-term transformation of the social structure. It is no good to entertain long disputations about "institutional revolution" over sirloin steaks and good red wines at small French restaurants in Harvard Square, while real and non-theoretical children, adolescents and adults are undergoing visible ordeal and literal starvation in the South End ghetto only two miles distant. This is the kind of random, unreal and irresponsible revolution that makes good literature and pleasant seminars, but does not compel a man to act right now upon the human desperation he sees before his eyes.

There is a certain kind of revolutionary courage, I believe, in fighting for a new world and still helping men to live without ordeal within the one that they are stuck with. In the remaining pages of this section, I am going to speak about a Free School that I know in which they do just that. It is a

Free School that is not intimidated by its own strong purchase upon time and history and does not feel the need to
make excuses for its own hard emphasis on strength and
power. It is a school in which the fear of domination and the
fear of excellence are not confused. It is a school, therefore,
which comes very close to what I think of as the ideal model
of the highly "conscious" Free School in the physical context
of an urban struggle, existing both outside the legal framework of the public schools and also outside of the framework
of the white man's counter-culture. It is not a well-known
school and I do not intend to make it better known. I will
not name this school, but I will try to give a sense of what it
is that makes me speak of it with so much admiration and to
remember it with so much hope and so much sense of ex-
pectation.

It is a school in which there are no more than six strong
teachers, eighty kids, a group of something like two dozen
active parents, a quiet, reserved, hard-working man of thirty-
one or thirty-two who is, at once, co-founder and Headmaster
of the school, another young person who is exclusively responsible for money-raising, visitors, the press. The young
man who began the whole thing in the first place, his seven
co-workers and their parent allies operate the Free School
as an honest and unique endeavor of their own creation, with
little apparent need to look for sanction on the outside.
The teachers are, for the most part, "political" people in the
sense that they obviously have a kind of framework, or a
way of looking at events, built up in part of hard street-logic,
in part of political actions, in part of just their human gut-
response to what they see around them in their daily work.
They do not, however, forget the lives of children in the
storm of words; nor do they place their ideologies or their

high-level goals in counterpoise to the immediate needs of intellectual and physical survival.

There is, within the school, a lot of emphasis on what the old-time teachers used to call "the basic skills." There is also a visible presence of high energy and fun, pupil irreverence and adult unprotectedness, none of that glaze and lacquer of "professional behavior" which is so often identified with the desexed and, as it often seems, dehumanized existence of the veteran teacher in the public system. There is, in its place, a warm, reassuring and disarming atmosphere of trust and intimacy and good comradeship between children and adults, a sense of trust that builds at all times on the recognition of the difficult conditions that surround their school and of the dangers which exist for each and every one of them on the outside.

There is also something in this school which is too rare in many of the Free Schools that I know: a real sense of stability and of sustained commitment in regard both to the present lives and to the future aspirations of the children in the school. It is a commitment which does not allow for sudden abdications, unannounced departures, TV appearances or visits to England and to Southern France on the part of these six teachers and their young Headmaster, but which on the contrary involves them in the most painstaking labor of medical referrals, legal battles, food-stamp hassles, landlord-tenant confrontations, difficult introductions and complex affiliations with more traditional independent schools and with rich people's colleges, job prospects and the like, all of which are the visible evidence and the daily confirmation of the fact that it is the survival of their children and not the slogans of the moment they believe in.

They do not have an eighteen-member Governing Board.

They do not have T-groups every Wednesday or Encounter Sessions on the weekend. They do not have beautiful girls from Vassar and dilettante poets from the other side of town coming over to "do marvelous things" and gather cocktail-party ammunition at the price of their own children. They DO teach reading to children who are illiterate and they have a remarkably good record of success. They do teach calculus and plane geometry to kids who want a chance someday to be an architect or engineer and not a janitor or garbage man or train conductor. They do, in certain situations, get extraordinarily mad about bad spelling. They will beat the shit out of any older kid who tries to get a younger kid involved with hard drugs. They do NOT believe that everyone has the right to do "his own thing." They do not believe that shooting heroin — or hooking someone else on heroin — is something anyone ought to be allowed to do. They are not afraid to give their kids direct instructions, straightforward criticism or precise and sometimes bitter admonitions. They like *Summerhill* but they do not think it is the only good book ever written. They do not hesitate to call a stupid piece of writing "stupid" or a piece of clear misinformation "false" or "wrong" out of the fear that A. S. Neill will come out of the plywood and accuse them of adult manipulation.

I have a sense of awe and reverence for the men and women who have put in three years of their lives in governing and teaching in this school. There are no quotations from the *I Ching* or Buckminster Fuller on the walls or in the stairways. There is none of that incessant jargon about Love and Joy, but there is a great deal of love and there is also a great deal of joy, not of the verbal and self-conscious kind which never gets past the point of mandatory glee, but love of the kind that men such as St. Francis and Tolstoi have spoken of: the love that turns, each day, from abstract concepts into an ethical vocation made of concrete deeds.

There is this also: an entire semester of consecutive and well-sustained math lessons and math exploration that grow out of a pre-planned period of observation at the local center of the drug trade . . . hours and evenings, weeks and days, for the better part of six months given over to a breakdown of the mathematics of police protection, cost for purchase, cost for sale of various kinds of white and yellow pills and stimulants and powders . . . the slow and merciless working-through of something that comes to be known among the children as the Heroin Equation . . . all of it based upon the profitable business then — and still, as of this writing — taking place within one house ten minutes distant from their classroom.

There is this: an entire semester of hard work, of writing, reading, research and the like — pre-planned and well-prepared and by no pretense either "undirected" or "spontaneous" or "accidental" — in the explication and examination of a set of old and evil regulation U.S. history textbooks, stolen or borrowed from a nearby public school . . . a strong and rich and long-sustained experience in the make-up and in the structure and substructure of political indoctrination and in the manufacture of a uniform body of apparent preferences and wishes in a nation's consciousness.

There is this: six months of labor, learning, exploration, physics, auto mechanics, chemistry and math, all growing out of a single, large, old automobile engine, chassis, gearshift, carburetor, muffler and the rest, taken from some old rusted and deserted car left in a nearby corner lot and dumped into the basement of the building where the Free School rents its rooms . . . the father of one of the children in the school leaving his work and taking off two afternoons each week, from two to four, and coming here from the auto-body shop across the square and spending those hours with a group of twelve or fourteen of the oldest children, teaching them how to take apart, examine and repair, then recon-struct that large and intricate and more-than-interesting piece of iron and steel.

There is this, too: a big tough black kid who perpetually struts and jeers and seems belligerent to you and to all other adults for two years, then suddenly one day sits down in the office of his teacher, of that same young man, that same young teacher who began the whole thing in the first place, and hustled the cash, and brought him in here from the street just three years back. He sits there now. The teacher sits there, and he looks this big tough black kid in the eyes and he tells him something that is going to circle in upon his consciousness a moment, then for a moment more, before he can quite grasp it, seize it, hold it in his hand. He tells him, quietly, that he has just won something that he desperately wanted. He did it, made it, won it, beat it, passed it, passed that goddamn long and fucking hard exam that he's been psyching out the whole long winter. He made it past the hardest thing he ever tried to do in his whole life. He's eighteen. He learned to read and write and do math and do logic and psyche out a long, incredible, stupid, evil, brutal and inescapable exam that he couldn't even have dared to think about just three years back, because he couldn't even have read the big BLOCK PRINT instructions on the cover. He did it this time, and he's sitting there now, six feet tall, two hundred pounds, and he begins to cry. His father's a janitor. His mother's a maid. He's going to enter college in September.

I have this strong and burning vision of the school I have

described. It is consistent. It is intense and vital. It is loyal to its children. It is like itself and does not try to be like any other school or to accommodate itself to any set of outside fashions. I hope they fight like Hell in future years to keep it like it is and not give in to all the shit that will descend upon their heads if they become well known.

FUNDING STRATEGIES:
SMALL FOUNDATIONS:
MIDDLE-SIZED FOUNDATIONS:
FORD, ROCKEFELLER, CARNEGIE

ONE TIME in a hundred, a Free School is adopted, almost from the first, by some umbrella organization like the Urban League. It does not happen like that very frequently, however, and most Free Schools therefore have to go the long, hard road of writing proposals, making direct appeals to countless individuals and corporations, figuring out the various Federal, state and local possibilities, and in general involving themselves in lots of complicated and exhausting ways with people whom they may not much admire but with whom they are obliged to talk, negotiate and sometimes literally beg for their survival.

A number of the more sophisticated but less realistic Free School people tend to believe that the struggle to achieve survival in these terms is, in some sense, self-compromising. Free Schools under black and Spanish parent sponsorship have had less hang-up on this subject, inasmuch as they have had more sane and visible knowledge of the needs and requisitions of survival. Too many of the young white Free School people that I know have come to the point almost of viewing survival of the school itself as just another obsolete and middle-class consideration, insisting instead that only some sort of "free," "organic," "unplanned" and "spontaneous" process can be trusted as a guiding principle or governing policy for the perpetuation and survival of the venture. The consequence of this is that large numbers of these "organic" and "spontaneous" Free Schools have come to their organic termination and spontaneous collapse in less than two years.

Survival in the Free School context has an order of importance only slightly secondary to that of truth and passion. There is a certain degree of bitterness, I think, about the process of bestirring hopes, exciting confidence and heightening loyalties and trust, then disappearing to Seattle, Sante Fe or San Francisco the next season, on pretext of the less than pure, ignoble and self-compromising danger of an application to the Ford Foundation or a visit from some meddlesome representative of the OEO. It is for this reason that I have included in the next few pages a number of passages of quite detailed suggestions in regard to money-raising. They may well strike some readers as intolerably orthodox, non-organic, non-euphoric, unspontaneous. There is, indeed, nothing organic about the folding and mailing of five hundred letters. There is nothing euphoric about the stealing, borrowing or lifting of somebody else's mailing-list. There is nothing in the least spontaneous about a visit to the ice-cold, anesthetic tower that contains the residential power-apparatus of the Ford Foundation. It is for just this reason that we ought to be prepared to struggle and to confront these kinds of hard and visible realities.

The tactical starting point for most of the Free School organizations I have known, is to obtain an appointment with the executive officer of one of the well-regarded, but not nationally significant foundations, the kind of foundation that gives away five, ten or twenty thousand dollars, not two hundred thousand. The man in charge of these foundations, in such cities as New York or Boston or St. Louis, is frequently a rather familiar type of academic gentleman: liberal and pleasant and congenial and relaxed, J. Press necktie, rolled-up shirt-sleeves, drawing from time to time upon a comfortable pipe of Cambridge consolation, conversant with phrases of the "child-centered process," "the Leicestershire Model" and such matters, but viewing these often less as subjects of real interest and belief, more as a nod to liberal dialect and as an amicable invitation not to view him as a total square.

Those who are not acquainted with the names and the locations of these small and middle-sized foundations can find the needed names, addresses, areas of special interest and the like in several different ways. There are, first of all, a number of states that publish a directory of local trust funds; in Massachusetts it is the office of the Attorney General that makes this list available. In other situations it is simple enough to find out the name and special focus of the most important of these small and middle-sized foundations by contacting some of the local lawyers, businessmen and civic leaders, in particular those who are identified with charitable causes. These people are often glad to offer useful contacts if they feel that we will, therefore, not bring pressure upon *them* for direct contributions. Liberal attorneys, in particular, in my experience, have brought to a high pitch the extremely difficult skill of holding onto their own money by telling you of twenty other men who have much more than they do. If this doesn't work, or if there are no well-known liberal attorneys in your town, it might be worth the investment of twelve dollars to obtain a large, if somewhat unwieldy, book published by the Russell Sage Foundation and giving the names of all foundations, charitable trusts and such. This publication, and a number of others like it, are listed in the final pages of this handbook.

The difficult task is not so much to get the names of the right places and the right foundations; rather, it is to break down those remarkable walls composed of ice-cold secretarial decisions, unanswered phone calls and incredible outer-office waiting areas that seem to stand on every side around the man who has the power to dispense the cash. In Boston and New York, those who are viewed as experts or professionals in fund-raising often recommend that you begin by mailing off an official-sounding, carefully budgeted and rather businesslike proposal. This is not good advice. It is much more effective to write a statement which does not attempt to imitate the standard language of the business world or of the government inter-office memo but which instead has the sound of your own voice, which is not loaded with all the stock expressions, and which draws specific and even challenging attention to the physical condition, educational injustice, economic deprivation of the children you are working with, as well as to some of the obvious and concrete goals of measurable skill-learnings. The best proposal of this kind that I have ever seen is Patrick Zimmerman's, written for the Southern School, in a poor-white Appalachian neighborhood of North Chicago. The address to write to, if you want to see a copy of this very good proposal, is included in the back part of this book.

The point is to be able to isolate our project in the mind of the efficient former banker, college dean or State Department officer who is now the program officer of the foundation, from all of the dozens of other letters, appeals and bureaucratic packages he sees each morning. It might not even be a bad idea to have the children write the letter to this gentleman in the first place, so long as they can get across the basic fact that you are asking him for money. LEAP School in New York City has a group of energetic kids known as the Hustle Committee. Their job is precisely to break down the bureaucratic walls and secretarial defenses that surround these foundation officers. They also join the teachers and the parents in the actual confrontation. Harlem Prep and several other schools in other cities do it in this manner also. It tends to transform the entire atmosphere within the corporation office, as well as to shake up the ordinary state of mind of those who work within it.

The first request, the original proposal, is generally so presented as to ask not permanent support but "starting money" or what are often known as "seed funds." There is a kind of screwed-up logic, as I find, in getting these first funds. The man we talk to generally wants to know what possibilities we have in mind for *subsequent funding* if he gives us the first grant. Nobody wants to make a significant donation to a school that will go under in six months. The crazy part of this is that all of our serious prospects for additional funding are often directly conditional upon the tentative approval of the man now sitting here before us. In Boston, for example, there is one highly respected and prestigious man whom I have known now for about five years and who has given a great deal of money to the Free Schools on a number of occasions precisely because we were prepared to say that we were convinced we could raise more from other people. The paradox of this is that once this well-known and extremely well-regarded man gives us the first donation, other individuals and small foundations start to give us funds as well, because they do not think he would do something stupid. It happens in other cities like this every time. You can't get A unless you tell him that you can get B through Z. The fact is that with A, you do get B through Z. Without, you don't. Whether the original statement is an optimistic lie or else a self-fulfilling prophecy, I do not know. I do know, however, that this much optimism is frequently the key to getting the first funds.

In one of the earlier sections of this handbook I have pointed out that it is necessary for a Free School to obtain nonprofit status in order to receive tax-free donations. It is not often possible to get this in Massachusetts in less than four months. In some states it is quicker; in others, somewhat longer. Free School people who are just starting out should know, however, that there are at least two ways in which to take in tax-free gifts before the tax-free status has been cleared. I do not know if this is possible in all states, but one device which has worked out in Boston and New York is to request some friends who are already incorporated on a tax-free basis for a school or pre-school or some other organization of this kind to "adopt" your project on a temporary basis as a secondary venture and to receive and forward money for you. The other shortcut, used more often in the Free Schools, is to ask your lawyer to apply for your nonprofit status and in the meantime to compose a letter which you then can show to those who ask, indicating as "advice of counsel" that you will receive nonprofit status and that you may, therefore, accept foundation gifts on a nonprofit basis. At the time when nonprofit status is approved, you then receive a number from the Internal Revenue Service which must be given to all foundations or individuals that request it for their own tax-records. This number — of great importance, as many unfortunate Free Schools discover about one-half-a-year too late — is also of use in buying books, equipment, furniture, lumber, paint and almost anything else without a sales tax. If for no other reason than to be aware of details of this kind, I think it is wise to seek out from the first a competent lawyer to stand with you, or to sit beside you, in the first few months of practical discussion, purchase and negotiation.

In the ultimate confrontation with the program officer at the small or middle-sized foundation, it has been my experience that people with my orientation, inhibitions, education, tend to waste an awful lot of time in trying to be well-mannered, trying to be civilized, trying to develop a sociable and unhostile atmosphere within the room, but somehow never getting to the real point. Many foundation officers are perfectly prepared to let us talk ourselves through an entire hour in this manner. Then they get up and nicely say: "Well, send me some more information in the mail."

It is difficult to do it — incredibly difficult in some situations — but it is of great importance not to waste time in sociable conversation but to get right to the point that you want cash, how much and for what purpose. For many white people, well-trained and tutored and "socialized," as I have been, in years of politic life and formal university preparation, it is almost an agony to break the atmosphere of indirection, look this agreeable but ultimately cool-headed and hard-thinking fellow in the eyes and ask him whether or not we get the money.

This is, perhaps, an excellent example of the situation in which a strong, articulate teen-age student can be of real help; either that, or else one of the bolder and more straightforward parents. I find that people who have been poor their whole lives waste less time than overbred Harvard men in getting to the real point. I've sat around sometimes for a full half-hour trying to arrow in on the real issue while the man behind the desk drew on his pipe and repeatedly turned the conversation off in various directions. At last the eighteen-year-old student sitting at my side looked at the bigwig in his broad-stripe shirt and pin-stripe suit and said: "Well, do we get the money, or don't we?" It is one of many situations in which I sense the psychological disadvantage of just those social contacts and those old-school-tie affiliations which, if I were on the other side of things, would be perhaps of a certain usefulness or, at the least, of sociable advantage.

There is a point which should be raised at this time and in this place and which, to some degree, may influence both the tone in which I offer the remaining portion of these funding strategies and the state of mind in which the reader listens to the things I say. It is rather easy, within the liberal shadowland of small foundations, Cambridge ladies and retired Harvard Deans who run the charitable trusts, to lose sight of the fact that what we do, if we do something serious and passionate and brave, is something which, in the long run, cannot logically be sustained, endorsed, empowered by these kinds of men and women. The Free School is established as our answer to an unjust order; yet the money which infuses small foundations, family charitable trusts, and Ford and Carnegie alike, is in itself one portion of that order, and the charitable trusts and the benevolent foundations in themselves constitute one elemental item in its superstructure. Large numbers of the executives in both the large and middle-sized foundations take, as it were, an interchangeable series of positions: this year with Ford, last year with OEO, next year with the

CIA . . . or back to Princeton . . . It does not require the reading of a left-wing radical polemic, nor even a particularly harsh and strident ideological position to look at the printed list along the masthead of the large or middle-sized foundation and to recognize there the names of just those men who plan our wars, control our armies, advise our presidents, govern our banks, hire our police and lay down the invisible demarcations of our ghettos. To ignore this point, and to assume that we are dealing, in the middle-sized and large foundations, with the antithesis of government and with the well-groomed representatives of the cheated and the poor, to assume that next year's Ford Foundation will be different from this year's CIA or last year's OEO is to exist in dreamland.

I find it difficult to speak of matters of this sort. There is no way, however, in which to work around the simple fact that something like irony, or deception, or bamboozlement, just has got to be at stake when poor and powerless people who are victims of the North American machine of exploitation, segregation and oppression go into the hallowed confines of a sleek and sweeping structure like the Ford Foundation and beg, on bended knee, for cash and freedom to escape the very interlock of anesthetic, air-cooled and unconscious desolation which this building in itself so perfectly exemplifies. Thinking of these things and understanding very well the silent and unspoken contradictions which are inevitably at stake in dealing with foundations, whether large or middle-sized or small, I still believe that we should work our hearts out to get money from these sources if we stand in any likelihood at all of real success. I just think we should go about it in a state of mind which is not cluttered with illusions and false expectations. I think we should be cognizant of the kind of chess match we are playing. I think that we should move our pieces with the calculation that this type of confrontation calls for.

SOLICITATION BY DIRECT MAIL:
CONTRADICTIONS, IRONIES, ILLUSIONS

THIS IS HOW some of the Free Schools put together a campaign for direct-mail solicitation. I have done it several times in Boston, and I have worked with others who were doing it in other sections of the country. It involves, in every case, a certain amount of luck and chance in terms of who you know or how you latch on to the types of names it takes to make the whole thing work. It also involves a number of the same kinds of inherent contradictions that are present in the applications, visits and proposals to the small and large and middle-sized foundations. I have heard black people in Boston speak of direct-mail solicitation as the strategy of persuading men and women in the suburbs to assist us in the process of denying them another generation of obedient maids and down-regarding butlers for their cocktail parties, spring cotillions, Christmas suppers, Passover dinners or tented celebrations at the Longwood Cricket Club. It is, I think, a little harsh when stated in these terms; and yet it is, in truth, a fair and reasonable description of the inner dynamics of the process of direct-mail solicitations. It is, for example, precisely to the kinds of social groups that I have just described that we attempt to send these letters and solicitations. In Boston, the most consistent and most generous support seems to come from the oldest, wealthiest and most aristocratic Yankee families; next, from the somewhat less affluent but often somewhat more committed Jewish families; third, from the much less affluent but, in many cases, steadfast and consistent people who are affiliated with the Unitarians, Quakers, peace organizations, Fellowship of Reconciliation and the like. I have also seen ingenious Free School people lift two dozen names from "sponsor lists" in theater-company or symphony-orchestra programs, from advertisements in the daily press (e.g., for BUSINESSMEN AGAINST THE WAR), from opera-company programs and from the Harvard Law School alumni mailing-lists.

I find that it does not do much good to send out huge mailings, for example to five thousand total strangers. It is also pretty useless to send out slick, printed or mass-duplicated letters. The best mailing-lists are those built up in large part upon word-of-mouth associations. I also think it is worthwhile, as I have said above in speaking of proposals, to try to steer away from liberal school-reform clichés and to figure out instead some unexpected ways by which to magnetize attention and to interrupt the routine process of unfolding letters, skimming them fast and dropping them into the nearest paper-basket. The most successful mailing I have ever done was one that involved no more than forty letters, one in which every person was addressed by name and one in which the first thing anybody saw on opening the flap was not a letter and not a printed booklet of whatever kind, but a pile of three or four large photographs of black, white, Spanish-speaking kids in action with their teachers and their parents in the Free School classroom. Eight thousand dollars was raised from just those forty letters. A year later, a mailing to eight hundred people of a "straight" letter, mass-duplicated and with no photographs, brought in less than one-half of that amount.

Here, as in the comments and suggestions that I made above in speaking of the large and middle-sized foundations, there is, I suppose, a kind of built-in contradiction. I speak of trying to write inspiring letters and to send a set of striking and attractive photographs. I also give voice, however, to a sense of skepticism in regard to motives and a sense of cynicism in regard to ultimate intentions in some of the men and women to whom we send our plea. I see no way to get around this basic paradox and often painful contradiction. There are dozens of individual good men in Boston, as in every other city of this nation. In the long run, however, the real question that we have to face is not so much how many decent and agreeable men we can enlist as intermediaries, but it is: *who controls the money?* The big money in Boston comes from banking, from insurance, from stock speculation, from years of foreign exploitation in the Third World, from investments in Nicaragua, Costa Rica, Panama, from the war-related industries such as those carried on by Raytheon and General Electric, from missiles and ball bearings, parts for rifles, parts for spaceships, parts for anti-personnel destruction weapons, as well as the kinds of vast and often limitless Federal subsidies that go to underwrite the preparation and the intellectual replication of such scholars, citizens and consultants as Walt Rostow, Henry Kissinger and William Bundy. There is also a vast amount of money in slum housing, liquor dealerships, police-supported drug transactions. These are the irreducible realities, in my belief, that stand about all tactical plans and all strategic thinking for the hustling of cash to subsidize a poor man's Free School.

It would be neglectful and unjust if I were not to frame the statements just preceding and those yet to come with the reiterated statement that there are, of course, large numbers of exceptional, loyal and courageous men in every city. Charles Merrill, Edward Yeomans and the late Bill Bender are just three of those in Boston who have been prepared to aid and further ventures even of those members of the oppressed classes with whose views and with whose ideologies they could not possibly agree. If Boston had about ten thousand men like Edward Yeomans and Charles Merrill, we would not have a congresswoman like Louise Day Hicks, a powerful landlord such as Mr. Gordon or a Chief Justice like Elijah Adlow. We do, however, and it is not by magic, accident or chance. It is because the wealthiest people in this city, by and large, are bigoted, cold and selfish human beings who honestly do not give a good goddamn what happens to poor children so long as they don't burn down the stores and houses that the rich men own, interrupt celebrations, marriages, graduations, polo matches or cotillions with their picket lines.

In working to raise money to support the Free Schools I believe in, I have been forced to learn, against my will, just what a hard and strong and ice-cold upper class it really is that pulls the strings in Boston. The major insurance companies are perhaps the worst: John Hancock prominent among them. Several of the major banks in Boston are, however, no less cynical in their operations. The First National Bank of Boston, closely identified as it is through personal affiliations with United Fruit on the one hand, and with the missile-industry of Cambridge and the suburbs on the other, spends a great deal of money to create a philanthropic image it has never merited. These statements are the necessary antidote to much of what has been written by conventional fund-raisers.

The inherent paradox and contradiction which I have attempted to describe in the preceding pages finds its most specific and dramatic manifestation in the timing of the direct-mail solicitation. The period of time that works the best is late November. This is not because Thanksgiving brings out the love and kindliness in the Board Chairmen and the Directors of the missile-industries and of United Fruit. It is because the tax year is approaching its termination in November and because it is the last chance for a man who has had earnings larger than his expectations to divest himself of surplus in the form of tax-exempt and charitable donations. Free School people who are working in the neighborhoods of the powerless and the poor sit down to write the most inspiring and most passionate funding-letters that they can; yet they do not deceive themselves as to the reason for the timing or as to the motive for the actual transaction. In the city of Boston, black and Spanish children simply do not live surrounded by a throbbing and compassionate mass of gentle-hearted landlords, liberal executives, guilt-ridden presidents of banks, investment firms and foreign-exploitation corporations. The amiable executive with his two-hundred-acre farm out in Still River, Massachusetts, and his Cake Box pipe-mix and his copies of *Transaction* and *The New Republic* on display out in the front hall or before the fireplace on the coffee table, may well be the most genteel and most reflective sort of fellow that four years of Exeter and four of Harvard can be expected to produce. In the long run, though, it is not possible to overlook the fact that he lives happily and well and with untroubled dreams within an all-white, segregated village, sends his two daughters off to an all-white, segregated prep school and votes each year *against* the referendum to redistrict for low-income housing in his own hometown. He is the same man who will surprise us with a check for fifteen hundred dollars in the third week of December. We receive it willingly, but without illusions.

POSTSCRIPT: No matter how much skill and how much strategy a group may use, every Free School sooner or later seems to reach a point of crisis where there simply is no money left to pay the bills or meet the monthly payroll. It is not surprising that this happens in so many cases; it is perhaps an index and reminder of the deep-down danger which we represent. It is surprising, however, to see the number of Free Schools which, in a situation of this kind, will secretly welcome the excuse to pin their inner loss of passion on an outside cause, and use the difficulties that they find in raising money as a credible reason to lock up the door and disappear for distant places. If you really do lose heart and want to disappear, at least be honest and admit the reason why. If the only reason is the lack of money, then it may be of some help to know a number of the things that have been tried in Boston and New York when Free Schools were in danger of collapse.

The best strategy I know, for Free Schools that are honestly on the verge of going under, is to go out into the neighborhood and round up all of the mothers and the fathers and the children and call them to a meeting and stand up before them and announce to them that you're in trouble: "We are out of cash. We don't have any money to pay salaries, or rent, or heat. We think that we will have to close for good." If the Free School has done something that is of real worth by this time, the neighborhood will not stand back and allow the school to die. People in the neighborhood themselves will go out and find money and make contacts and approach the churches and approach the ministers and approach the rich men or rich women that they know. This has happened in Boston several times, but one time in particular that I recall.

The Free School teachers and the Free School parents discover that they are out of money and that they cannot meet their obligations. In this emergency they go out into the streets and pass out fliers both in English and in Spanish. They walk into the projects and into the local bars and liquor stores and Puerto Rican restaurants and soul-food places and the corner grocery stores. The flier says that they are in real trouble, that they do not want to close and that they do not want the children to arrive there in the morning to confront an empty building and a boarded door. They pass out those fliers in the morning and in the afternoon. At eight at night the place is flooded with the largest crowd of neighborhood people who have ever come here. In years of organizing and in months of work to draw in neighborhood people, they never have had a turn-out of this size, until they were in trouble.

The neighborhood people, many of them, reach right into their pockets and their pocketbooks and wallets. Others go out to talk at local churches Sunday morning before services begin, and others go off and hold out buckets in the path of college kids at Harvard and at M.I.T. By one means or another they bring in about five thousand dollars. This seems to me a very stirring and important passage of experience. The Free School learns that it has won its way into the hearts of these poor people. Henceforth, the Free School will not be allowed to close, not even if the parents and the teachers should lose heart and wish to do so.

The other approach that sometimes does the job as well

is to get on the phone and call the press, and get them in there with the TV cameras and the education writers and the rest, and sit right down with several of the parents and with several of the children at your side, and tell those TV cameras that you are about to close — and also tell them why. The announcement of immediate extinction is often an excellent way to raise ten thousand dollars. The same idea, but on a somewhat smaller scale, is to pick out the names of ten or twenty of the people who have helped you most over the course of years and write them an extremely candid letter. I have done this once on the eighteenth or the twentieth of June. The letter contains about ten sentences and winds up with these words: "If you still think of yourself as part of the struggle of black people for their liberation, and if you have enough money in the bank to go off on a summer's holiday or on a summer's cruise, will you please write us a check before you go? If you do not, we will not be here still when you come back." The letter carries a postscript: "This letter is being mailed to fifteen people."

The letter excited no response in nine out of these fifteen people; the other six sent in four thousand dollars. In certain instances, I know very well that one or another of these methods of approach will not be possible. In some situations, the press idea or the neighborhood idea will just not work. In others, the letter-writing strategy will not be feasible. The point I want to make is just that we should not lie down in silence and consent to die. If the Free School starts up and then finds that it cannot survive, it is a metaphor of failure for the people in the neighborhood and on the block. The perseverance of the Free School, on the other hand, is like a symbol of enthusiasm, strength and continuity for those who pass it daily on their way to work and who entrust their children to its care. I think this is one reason why the people in the neighborhood that I have just described would not allow the Free School on their block to die.

RESEARCH AND EXPLOITATION:
LIVING OFF THE SURPLUS OF
THE UNIVERSITIES

IN THIS SECTION I am going to speak about the exploitation-in-reverse of some of the major universities and of some of the major research organizations: those, in particular, which always and forever seem to be "exploring" and "researching" into ghetto neighborhoods in order to gather statistics or to test out theories. The kind of tactic that I have in mind represents the turning of the tables on the part of people who are powerless and poor against the people who are experts in the explication of their poverty and impotence. It might be described as the strategy of getting research people to run interference for the much less influential and much less prestigious Free School people in obtaining government or foundation funds and then in making them available not for research into, but for sustenance of, the Free School operation.

In order to explain this to people who are unfamiliar with the social research process and with the remarkable universe of men like Daniel Moynihan and Nathan Glazer, it is necessary to explain a basic fact of life within the intellectual and university world of New York, Boston and Chicago. It is very difficult, often impossible, to raise the money to feed people who are starving. It is much, much easier to obtain sufficient funds to maintain twenty pink and plentiful research scholars in the style to which a research scholar learns to be accustomed in order that they may spend six years or more compiling evidence and statistics as to the "possible ill effects" of mass starvation. This seeming paradox is no paradox at all as soon as one begins to understand that research of this kind does not exist in order to diminish pain or to alleviate despair, but to extend the barriers of knowledge, to expand the frontiers of pure learning and, in the meantime, of course, to keep the children of the social scientists in all-white, or in nearly all-white, upper-class private schools and to maintain their wives in pretty shoes and handsome dresses from Design Research and Lord and Taylor.

I remember a grant of eighty thousand dollars that was used by men at Harvard, four years back, to interview hundreds of young black people in the Boston Schools in order to find out if they liked their schools, if they considered themselves to be in good condition, intellectually and psychologically, and to find out in general how they looked upon their prospects. As their schools decayed, their lives collapsed and their prospects turned to jail and heroin, the research people kept on taking down the data and the tape recorders kept on spinning. Nobody ever intervened to make a difference in the misery of any child, but a number of men went home at night to beautiful places out in Lexington and Lincoln on the money that they picked up from their expertise. It got so that they could make two hundred dollars in a day retailing stories they had learned by listening to their interviewees on the tape recorders. For the same money, of course, they could have begun and run a marvelous school and changed the lives of those two hundred children, but that would not have been accepted as "pure research."

It is not difficult, then, to understand the bitterness that people in the black community express at gross and obvious intellectual exploitation of this kind. In several of the Free Schools during 1968 and 1969, it was possible to find more probing, poking, smiling, questioning, note-taking, tape-making, photo-snapping research scholars, Master's candidates and bored professors from the Harvard Graduate School of Education than children, mothers, fathers or their teachers. The black reaction to this ritualistic sucking of the blood has been at once ingenious and inventive. It did not take long before the black community leaders, in and of themselves, and the parents and the teachers of the Free Schools, in particular, began to understand the ironical implications of the process taking place. The Free Schools do not really "need" the research scholars with their cumbersome tape recorders, cameras, video-tape machines and what not. The research scholars, however, need the Free Schools and the ghetto that surrounds them or they have no occupation. Without the ghetto, without starvation, without cultural and social "deprivation," without legal and educational discrimination, there could be no Nathan Glazer and no Arthur Jensen and no Daniel Moynihan. Without the Free Schools there could be no Harvard Education courses in BLACK RADICAL ALTERNATIVES TO PUBLIC EDUCATION. There could be no hundred-thousand-dollar grant for research into POSSIBILITIES OF STATE-SUPPORTED EDUCATIONAL ALTERNATIVES WITHIN THE INNER CORE. Master's candidates at Harvard, Boston University, Simmons, Tufts and Boston College would not have any places to go to research their term papers. Thesis writers would have to write the same dull papers that their teachers and professors wrote before them. Video-tape experts would have nobody to tape and clip and edit and record.

The Free Schools in this area, therefore, and now in Chicago and New York and several other areas as well, have gathered together in an effort to attempt to turn the Free Schools into something of a "closed shop." In Boston, under the aegis of the Black United Front, there is now an organization which functions as a "research review" committee. The committee examines all applications for research within the Roxbury, South End and Dorchester communities and gives permission only to those research programs which are not only to the clear advantage of the children in the schools in question but which are also ready to disburse at least one-tenth of research funds to help to subsidize the watchdog labors of the Black United Front. This seems to me a strong, effective and vigorous response to such gross and exploitative processes as have for so long gone unchallenged. In New York City, in the start of June of 1971, a group of teachers, parents and students from ten or fifteen different coalition-groups in several cities met to consider the application of this tactical approach on a much broader basis. The discussions led to a concerted plan to work out the specific details prior to the spring of 1972.

The intention here is not to establish some sort of vicious or totalitarian stranglehold on free exchange of information. Nor is there any sense of personal dislike toward those within the intellectual communities who have been friends and boosters of the Free Schools. The idea is not retaliatory, retrogressive or vindictive. It is realistic, logical and forward-thinking. The basic rule of thumb for oppressed peoples, in a time of social revolution, is not to go out into the hills and manufacture rifles of their own, but to place hands upon the weapons of the oppressor and skillfully to turn those weapons in his own eyes. The research process, in the field of social change and social struggle at the present

period in the United States, is the weapon of choice by which
the privileged classes have been able to postpone almost
all solemn, honorable and risk-taking action in the guise of
gathering "further information," accumulating greater quan-
tities of "more conclusive data" precisely in those areas within
which they already have a high degree of certitude but little
will to pay the price that transformation calls for. It is a
great deal easier to obtain one hundred thousand dollars to
do a research study on THE FEASIBILITY OF THE ESTABLISH-
MENT OF A COMMUNITY-ORIENTED FREE SCHOOL IN THE INNER
CORE than it is to get the same amount of money and to use
it to operate a school that you have already set up.

It is not difficult from this to gain the powerful impression
that the true purpose of research is not to determine the
proper steps that must be taken in order to go about a realistic plan of action but rather to keep a number of intelligent people occupied for a reasonable period of time with a
plausible sense of honorable intention and, at the same time,
to maintain them with a reasonable income. Like it or not,
this is the nation that we live in. Hundreds of thousands of
dollars are available for looking into "feasibilities," "aspects,"
"implications," but often not a dime for payroll or survival.
The method of response that I now have in mind, and one
which is now in process of execution by large numbers of
the Free School organizers and fund-raisers, is not to wait for
the approach and inquiry from research organizations or the
local universities, but to go right to them and to ask them
flatly if they will cooperate. It is not difficult at all to assign
a portion of each of the major salaries within a Free School,
or even a certain portion of the operating expenses of the
total organization, to a research project which is already in
existence. It is also possible to create a research project

precisely for this purpose. In a sense, when this takes place, what we are doing is to use "feasibility funds" to render somewhat more feasible a program which is already in existence. It is, for sure, a roundabout way to finance a real program; yet it is being done, in more or less this fashion, at the present time, in several of the Free Schools in the Eastern cities, and several of the significant salaries within these schools are being subsidized in just this way. In a sense, I guess what I am saying is that every school of education, "Urban Studies Institute" or such, with major research funds, ought to be looked upon by Free Schools as a possible conduit to or from the Federal government or to or from the large foundations. I know that I have antagonized some of my academic friends by making unconventional and, from their point of view, impractical recommendations of this kind. What is more interesting, though, is the surprising number of those who have been willing to cooperate.

FOOTNOTE ON EXPLOITATIVE RESEARCH: Two years ago, in Boston, I was contacted by a woman doing research at the Harvard-M.I.T. "Joint Center for Urban Studies." She said that she wanted to interview me on a matter related to "the financial situation" of the Free Schools. When I pressed her for the purpose of her research, I was told that her objective was to look into the difficulties that the Free Schools find in trying to raise money. She said that she wanted to talk with me in order to find out the amount and nature of the financial help we were or were not receiving from big business. I asked her how much money she and her co-workers were receiving to look into how much money we were *not* receiving. She said that they had just received a charitable grant of $45,000 to look into this. I asked her where the money came from, and she named a well-known trust fund in the Boston area. The trust fund that she named was one to which, on several occasions during the course of four years, we had made an application. At no time had they granted us more than a fraction of the sum this research group had now been given.

I replied to her, then, that two of my co-workers and I would be willing to have an interview with her on this subject. I said that our price would be five hundred dollars. She said that this suggestion was "somewhat unusual" and that she would be forced to check with her superiors. I did not hear from her again.

REHAB HOUSING: FRANCHISE OPERATIONS: WAREHOUSE BOOKSTORE

THE TACTICS of the genteel shakedown, in regard to research organizations, universities and such, transforms the Free School state of mind somewhat from one of plea, petition and polite knee-bending into the attitude of self-support or, at the least, of self-protection. This raises the stakes a bit and leads into one rather different recommendation that I would like to offer.

The question arises as to why the Free School spends so much of its scarce time and labor in pursuit of funds which have been earned by others instead of devising the means by which to earn those funds ourselves. The point has been made, by several of those who have been involved in matters of this nature for the past six years, that some of us put as much time, labor, worry, sweat into the work of *begging* for these funds as other people might put into *earning* them. The point is also made that starting a school cannot be infinitely less subtle nor a great deal less complex than starting a small business operation. If we can do one, why should we not attempt to do the other? Do we consider ourselves to be less competent, less skilled or less consistent in our patterns of work than the landlords who receive our rents, the bookstore owners who extract our dollars from us, the men

who run the places that we go to after work to get our doughnuts and hamburgers? These questions, of course, and the
whole bent of this discussion, inevitably set off a lot of criticism, anger, skepticism and resistance in some quarters.

To many men, the whole idea of Free School self-support
sounds too much like an imitation of the landlords we condemn or of the men who operate the "rip-off" groceries
and liquor stores along Columbus Avenue in the South End.
If the idealistic, gentle and utopian children of the counter-
culture look with reservation on a visit to the Ford Foundation or to the OEO, their sense of reservation is all the more
intense and strong in the face of the idea of running our own
profitable business: "I didn't come here into the South End
to do what my old man does back in Scarsdale."

It is hard to make this clear and not grow cynical ourselves, but in my opinion there is a very good argument to
be presented for doing just what this young white man or
white woman most abhors. In simple truth, and in the long
run of events and consequences, either we do what his old
man does back in Scarsdale, only on our terms and by our
code of moral values, or else we ask his father to keep on
with it himself, but share the profits with us in the form of
charitable donations. This is, in fact, what all of traditional
money-raising is about. The good white radical kid who does
not want to soil his hands in "exploitative business practice"
just does not stop to ask where all the Free School money
comes from in the first place. Every dollar, every dime and
every penny in an unjust nation is, in some fashion, "impure"
or "contaminated" or "immoral." The question is whether
the Free School keeps on begging for the proceeds of injustice or whether it learns the way to earn those proceeds on
its own and in its own terms.

Each of the strategies for money-raising that I have described above, no matter what the state of mind or sense of leverage that we are prepared to bring to bear, derives in one sense or another from a candid recognition of our own essential weakness in the face of those who have the cash and power. In turn, these processes both highlight and intensify that sense of weakness by inviting outside supervision and evaluation. No matter what we say to one another on this score, and indeed no matter what we say by way of personal bravado to those men and women who come in to visit and to look us over on behalf of major corporations and foundations, there is the quiet recognition at all times, both on our side and theirs, of the real relationship in which the Free School people stand before those who can grant us longer life or else can force us to close down. The Free School depends upon the benefaction of the rich. The benefaction of the rich rests on an unjust order. The perpetuation of that order rests upon the maintenance and replication of the present patterns of indoctrination and mass alienation carried out in various ways but, more than any other, by the universal patterns of required attendance in the public schools or else in those institutions which are able to provide a parallel experience. No man, no industry, no social class, no large foundation, no government agency, no ruling power on the face of earth will ever agree to subsidize its demolition. Industry is not in business to lose customers. Ford and Carnegie do not exist to free their denizens and clients from the agencies of mass persuasion. These points are unmistakable and obvious to all who know the ropes within the black and Spanish-speaking Free Schools. If they are not often stated, it is because they are at all times in the air.

In order first to win and then to hold on to the cash and
backing of rich people, as well as of corporations and the big
foundations, the Free School has to be definable as something
less than "provocation" or "subversion." This means that
either the Free School needs to learn to be dishonest and
conceal its own most serious intentions, or else it means that
people in the Free School have to learn to trim their sails and
be, in fact, less conscientious and less passionate than they
wish to be. In ordinary practice, both these processes take
place in every Free School. It is therefore of deepest urgency
that we begin right now to think about a number of new
and stronger ways in which to earn the cash we need to keep
these Free Schools open. In the past two years I have listened
to a dozen well-developed schemes for Free School self-support. In the following pages I am going to present three of
those plans which seem to me to make the most sense. Each
of these notions has been worked out at some length with
several Free School leaders in New York and Boston.

1. REHAB HOUSING

There are a number of reasons why the idea of rehab
housing is, right now in 1972, a logical and realistic venture
for a Free School in a black or Spanish-speaking neighborhood. Landlords in the ghetto neighborhoods are at this
point very much on the defensive in the face of militant
pressure from well-organized tenant co-ops and from such
agencies as the Urban League and NAACP. In every city
there are landlords in positions so invidious, awkward and
increasingly unprofitable as to be ready to sell out or, in
some cases, just to *get out*. Many desert their buildings and

just disappear. There is no reason why a Free School with community affiliations ought to sit back and watch while the city clears these lots or else allows investors to come in and turn old houses into high-rent units for rich people. There is also a certain amount of Federal money still available for the rehabilitation of low-income housing. In some cases, it is available as an outright grant. In others, it is available as a long-term loan at 3 percent. I have in mind a number of black and Spanish-speaking men in Boston who are good carpenters, brick-layers, master electricians and, in two instances, architects and engineers. Rehab housing is not a hip or whimsical idea for picking up a couple of hundred dollars in a year by selling Indian headbands on the fringe of Harvard Square or running a not-for-profit coffee house in Palo Alto. It is, on the contrary, a down-to-earth and realistic means of bringing the Free School into direct contact with the incipient resources of its own community, to do so in a manner which can seriously involve the older students in apprenticeship relationships with carpenters, electricians, engineers, to do so moreover in ways which ask not only physical labor but also math and reading, physics, electronics and a number of other academic skills, while at the same time we are building a strong base of large-scale funding for the Free School. Indianapolis, Boston, Philadelphia and New York are all potential settings for this type of venture. There are enough skills, resources, areas of hard expertise already present in the black communities of these cities to make the initial venture feasible and not entirely unfamiliar. Whether it works from that point on depends on our ability and will to do the job at least as well as those within the power structure whom we now condemn.

2. FRANCHISE OPERATIONS

There are, at the present time in the United States, several dozen well-known and successful franchise operations. Many of these corporations do a large part of their business in the neighborhoods of the black and poor but feed back very little of the profit that they make. Two of the most obvious examples of this kind of corporation are the short-order food-chains owned and operated by MacDonald's and by Colonel Sanders. Each of these operations brings in profits in the area of twenty-five to fifty thousand dollars for a single outlet in a single year. There are other large franchise-corporations which can bring in equally substantial profits. Len Solo suggests, for example, that a Free School might well earn a large part of its payroll from the operation of a Brigham's ice cream stand in Boston, a Texaco or ESSO station in some other sections of the country, or a franchise laundromat in almost any section. Each of these options represents a certain degree of "rip-off" in the minds of those who are prepared to see a Marxist revolution taking place on Monday morning but none of them represents a product or a service which is going to do specific harm to other human beings.

The major advantages of the franchise operation are as follows: (1) It represents the kind of work that can be learned in a short time. (2) It involves a minimum of complex dealings with wholesalers, middlemen and such. (3) It brings in large and stable profits. The challenge here is less in the matter of the day-to-day work of operation, more in the initial push and pressure it is going to take to win the franchise in the first place. There is one reason at least to expect that some of the more prestigious corporations will be willing to look with favor on the right kind of approach. Most of these franchise businesses have been all-white in ownership and orientation for a long, long time. They are, at present, therefore, like the ghetto landlord, very much on the defensive. It may well take a concentrated publicity campaign against one corporation or another in order to create the situation which will open up a number of new franchise opportunities; this is, however, the sort of thing at which Free Schools are good. If we know nothing else, we know at least how to get out the press. In New York, one of the Free Schools is already making plans to open up a franchise ice cream parlor. During the next year, there is going to be a lot of joint discussion among a number of the Free Schools in this section of the country in order to settle on a single corporation for a concentrated push.

3. WAREHOUSE BOOKSTORE

The warehouse bookstore is the single recommendation that the people in the Free Schools tend to view as most exciting and least formidable. This is because it deals with a commodity of sale which we already deal with in our daily work and therefore do not look upon as unfamiliar. It does, however, call for an immense amount of realistic calculation in advance. I do not, for example, believe that many of the Free School groups I know would be prepared to handle the incredible complexities and intricate details of a conventional bookstore. I also know that conventional bookstores are exposed to very great loss from theft and vandalism. The recommendation that some of us have in mind, therefore, is not to run an ordinary bookstore, with its complex overhead and its immense back-order file, but rather to run a

very special kind of operation which competes with univer-
sity- and college-operated bookstores in a rather narrow, but
extremely profitable, category: standard titles, texts and
trade books both, but only those titles which are scheduled
for the large and popular and well-known college lecture
courses.

Those who have been out of college for ten years may not
be aware of the very large classes that now take place at
such institutions as Northeastern, Harvard, Boston University and Boston College. Hundreds of classes in several
universities like these involve between two hundred and
two thousand pupils. In each class there may be something
like ten, fifteen, twenty standard, mandatory or suggested
titles. In certain subject areas, those, for example, having to
do with current topics, social unrest, urban studies and the
like, there is a standard and uninterrupted market in the
Boston area for ten or twenty thousand copies of particular
titles. I am suggesting, then, that what we ought to do is work
directly with some of the liberal and more-than-liberal
professors at these major universities, ask them to help us
in advance with lists and titles and also to urge their pupils
to give all of their business in these subject areas exclusively
to us, and not to bring it to the college bookstore.

The set-up, then, might be less like a formal bookstore,
more like a warehouse operation in some easily accessible
location, where the books are stocked and where the college
representatives would come to pick up numbered cartons
of the titles that they want. Boston is, of course, an ideal
place to do this. There are so many college students in the
metropolitan region that several warehouse operations of
this kind might flourish at the same time. The same, I think,
would be the case in New York, in Chicago or in San

Francisco, as well as in a number of other cities with large college populations. Students look without much love upon the college-operated bookstores and I should think large numbers would be glad to help a Free School stay alive by ordering most of the standard and expensive books from us. There is, moreover, a certain degree of poetic justice in the thought of ordering hardcover books and paperback titles by such men as Malcolm X, Franz Fanon, Eldridge Cleaver, Ivan Illich, Oscar Lewis, John Gerassi, Piri Thomas, Edgar Friedenberg, John Howard Griffin, Paul Goodman, Howard Zinn, James Baldwin, Truman Nelson, Lee Lockwood, Erik Erikson, George Dennison, Tolstoi, Thoreau, Emerson, Gandhi, Lenin, Trotsky and St. Francis — not from the antiseptic, turnstyle-operated, TV-camera-circulating college bookshop, but from the mothers and the fathers and the teachers and the black and Spanish-speaking children of the streets of Boston, New York and Chicago, who are, in fact, the spiritual heirs of Malcolm and the brothers of Franz Fanon and the intellectual inheritors of St. Francis, Tolstoi and Thoreau.

I am certain now, after speaking with several of the men who run the major bookstores in New York and Boston, that a warehouse distribution-center of the kind I have in mind, if wisely managed and carefully established in the minds of a number of the well-known university figures in advance, can earn for a Free School as much as fifty thousand dollars in a year. This is one-half the total budget of some of the Free Schools. There is an organization here in Cambridge which is prepared to offer free and immediate business counsel to any Free School that would like to try to open such an operation. I have given the name, address and contact for this organization in the back part of this book.

COURT SUITS: VOUCHERS: LEGAL
STRATEGIES: SUING THE SYSTEM
FOR A CHILD'S LIFE

THIS IS THE FINAL SECTION on fund-raising. I am not going to describe here another practical approach to Free School funding but am going to speak instead about the long-range legal implications of a new idea that has been talked about a great deal in the last two years within the black communities of Boston and New York. It has been called by some a constitutional lawyer's reconception of the voucher scheme. It has also been described as the consumer advocate's version of the same idea: perhaps this is the most precise description. It is, in essence, an ethical and legal argument for the public's right to sue, in pedagogic terms, for "truth in packaging," and to demand and to collect appropriate recompense when the label is not honest or when the contents are not as they have been advertised.

The discussion begins with a flood of seminars, essays, speeches, recommendations, from a number of different scholars in the past two years — those who are as influential and well-respected, for example, as Christopher Jencks, on the one hand, and Ivan Illich on the other. These essays, writings, recommendations have begun, for the first time, to focus the thinking of large numbers of the Free School people on the rather unfamiliar and hard-boiled question of ex-

actly what a year of school is "worth" or what it is supposed
to have been "worth" in terms of cash expended, skills delivered, learning undertaken and credentialized reward made
possible. Extended intellectual debate and disputation in regard to vouchers has prompted a number of otherwise idealistic and non-mercenary individuals to think no longer exclusively in terms of educational depth and wisdom, freedom,
openness and inquiry and creativity and such, but also in
the terms of something as specific and non-idealistic as delivery of skills which have been advertised and promised by
the public schools but which, in certain situations, have not
ever been delivered.

This is the kind of logic that I now hear: It is written,
claimed, reported, documented and accepted in most quarters as unquestioned fact, that a year of public school, by
present allocations and financial patterns — geographical,
physical and such — is measurably short-changing children
of poor people. If this seemingly obvious statement can in
fact be statistically confirmed, and if it can be established,
in addition, that the failure of public school to have been able
to deliver certain areas of basic skill means direct, obvious and
measurable economic disadvantage and specific loss of real
competitive power for a child who must go to school in
Watts or Roxbury or Harlem; if, moreover, these things
can be tested and confirmed and even calibrated, in the very
terms of numbers, tests and test-scores which this school
system rests its expertise upon, as well as of other measurable
items such as expenditures per-pupil for the academic year,
years of teacher-preparation, tenure and experience, money
spent as well on other personnel, equipment, books, supplies
and all the rest, then it seems to many people, as it does
equally to me, that thousands of young black men and young

black women, ages fourteen to twenty, twenty-two or twenty-four, have a good strong case to sue the public schools they have attended for the loss of childhood, for early crippling, for injury sustained while in the place of work, for cutting-out of hearts and breaking of the knees, blinding and marbling of eyesight, blood on the lip and ruin on the brow. In other words, they ought to sue the schooling system for their own lives.

This proposition, strange as it sounds and melodramatic as it may at first appear, has met with more sustained, intense, impassioned, realistic, legal-tactical-strategic approbation, affirmation and response than any idea pertaining to the public schools or Free Schools that I have ever presented to a group of my co-workers, whether in a white man's seminar or in a poor man's meeting-hall. It ought to be possible to prove, not with polemic or by emotional presentation, but by all hard statistics and from all cold and reputable sources, that in black neighborhoods, during the years from 1955 to 1965, or even up to 1970 in some sections of the nation, before the period at which the schools began to be harassed by militant rights-groups and to rush in lots of superficial changes and at least apparent dollar-increments to buy off bullets, during that time the sheer expenditure of cash, as measured in health services, library expenses, teacher-pay and building upkeep and the rest, was often one-third or one-half less than what it was in all-white or in almost all-white areas. In Boston this charge of direct and measurable cash-discrimination is substantially confirmed in documentations gathered and in publications printed by the NAACP and A.D.A. It is confirmed in a more general way in publications signed and authorized by men such as Erwin Canham, Lewis Weinstein, Richard Cardinal Cushing and Ralph Lowell, to name only four of the least polemical and most quietly respectable leaders of the white community of Boston in the 1960s. If we consider, as well, some additional matters, which are possibly more important than mere cash-investment, for example the attitudes and staffing and the kinds of grotesque textbooks used throughout the 1950s and the 1960s, I think that a good case of poison contents and dishonest labels might well be presented in a court of law.

In most suburban schools surrounding major cities, it is correct and realistic to suggest that almost any child knows that he can go to college, or to something with the approximate economic payoff of a college, so long as he sits still and smiles quietly in the back seat of a classroom for twelve years in sequence. He has to be a little special *not* to make it. In poor and black North Dorchester and Roxbury, as well as in many black, poor-white and Spanish-speaking neighborhoods of New York and Philadelphia and St. Louis and Chicago and Milwaukee, the student who has been processed first within a school such as the Christopher Gibson or the Garrison or the Howe, then on to places like the Martin Luther King and then Dorchester High, has got to be exceptional even to stand a slender chance to break out of the process of menial-labor manufacture *which is in fact the real creative occupation of the urban school.*

Liberal intellectuals are frequently afraid to speak of this. They are afraid that, by pinpointing consequences of this kind, they may appear to buttress or sustain the implication of inherent biological or family-oriented liabilities proposed by men like Moynihan or Jensen. It is, however, an irrefutable, if agonizing, fact that poor kids in this nation have been technically retarded in a thousand measurable ways by public education. A man — teacher, citizen or judge — has only to visit in the cities and in the suburbs for the littlest period of time to recognize the dazzling and inexorable gulf of quality and standards. Either black people are dull, slow-witted, stupid and inferior, or else their schools are murderous. There is no third choice. I take the second option. If all schoolchildren, in certain moral, psychological and utopian terms, are in an intellectual and custodial Hell within the public schools, still we know very well there is a difference between a glass-walled, smooth, successful Hell like those we see in Evanston and Darien and New Rochelle, and the kind of misery, rage and chaos, technological ineptitude and pedagogic clumsiness in schools of Harlem, Roxbury and Cleveland. The same child, with the same yearnings, brains and feelings, possibilities, potentials, in a black school of Boston, Newark, Philadelphia, at the age of seventeen, is likely to be on a par with white kids out in Darien of age eleven, twelve or thirteen. Values, taste and culture don't have anything to do with what I mean. In terms of figuring out how much you really end up paying for something that you badly want to buy, or saying precisely what you mean when what you mean is something complicated and not often said, or figuring out a very difficult, intricate and profoundly involuted piece of writing which, for your purposes and personal needs, you desperately wish to understand, in terms like these the kids I have in mind are measurably cheated. They know it. Their folks know it. Their white racist School Boards know it. Only their liberal friends are scared to say it.

Therefore, when Bill Owens, a strong and militant black man in this city, decided a couple of years back that he was going to sue the City of Boston for his own children, and if they wanted, for the children of his neighbors — sue the city for the education they had coming to them but did not receive — I thought this was a very eloquent idea and I began to wonder if more people and more organizations could not do this also. Bill Owens took his children out of public school and put them instead into one of the parent-operated Free Schools. He then demanded that the city pay him for that school because he knew that they were dying in the school that they had previously attended. He was right. He had — and has — a very strong case. Still, I do not see lawyers from the various respectable liberal organizations rushing in to his support. I ask myself: Why don't these older and prestigious civil libertarians support his struggle? Is the life of a child less subject to litigation than a broken arm or broken collarbone or twisted elbow? Or is the problem, rather, that these powerful lawyers recognize only too well that Bill Owens has hit upon a very dangerous idea, one that might well begin to cause this educational apparatus serious trouble if we start to take it seriously. It will, for sure, because it gets right down to the gut-level issue not just of racist education but of the present school-fraud altogether. School *doesn't* deliver what it promises and advertises, and *does* deliver something poisonous and vicious that it never mentions on the label. Bill Owens' drive to sue the city for his child's life is a revolutionary's version of the voucher system. It is a blood-filled, passionate, loving and aggressive adaptation, in guerrilla terms, of the more complex and more mechanical structure of reallocation dreamed up by the men in Washington and Cambridge.

In the present period (winter and spring of 1972), a number of people in the Free Schools of New York, Chicago, Washington and other cities in the East are beginning to talk a lot about Bill Owens' action. They are beginning to speak about "class suits" and "neighborhood suits" to repossess the educational tuition that could subsidize the strong and viable alternatives to public classrooms which these parents have created or are now creating. In recent months, a number of the people at the Harvard Center for Law and Education have become involved in various discussions that have to do with this idea. I have given their names and ways to reach them in the pages of leads, contacts and addresses that conclude this handbook. In the months ahead, if there are groups of parents, teachers or attorneys who would like to begin to act upon this notion, I would like very much to be in touch with them and I would welcome correspondence with them.

POSTSCRIPT

THERE IS ONE other method of fund-raising which I did not mention in the earlier pages of this book. This is the method of writing a little book to share some of the struggles and some of the challenges and some of the details that a Free School needs to deal with. This is, of course, one of the major motives for the publication of this handbook. My wife and I intend to share the proceeds from its sale with several of the Free Schools that we know firsthand, admire and believe in. Those who would like to add their own small offerings to ours are invited to send nonprofit contributions to The Education Action Fund, Inc., P.O. Box 27, Essex Station, Boston, Massachusetts, 02112, a tax-exempt trust which will distribute funds to a dozen different ghetto-centered Free Schools in five cities. It would be a quiet way of helping decent people in all sections of the country to fight for the lives and for the liberation of their children.

Contacts, Leads, Addresses

FREE SCHOOLS:
CONTACTS, LEADS, ADDRESSES

IN THE FOLLOWING PAGES I am going to outline, as concisely as I can, the major contact-points — in terms both intellectual and geographical — which seem to me to indicate the breadth and depth of Free Schools in this nation. It is not a definitive bibliography or anything of that kind. It is more like a set of "Yellow Pages" for the Free Schools. I hope it will be of help to those who are attempting to begin their own schools and do not know where to look or how to set forth for advice and funds and all the rest. I have not tried to limit this list of leads and contacts to the books or organizations which reflect my own ideas or viewpoints. Some do support my views, some don't, and some support them but raise doubts and questions which I have not spoken of within this handbook. In my belief, an exciting Free School represents neither a single uniform viewpoint, nor a bland and non-directive obfuscation of all viewpoints, but rather a strong and uninhibited ferment of competitive viewpoints and of competitive provocations. I hope the following pages, in counterpoise to the writing in the pages of the book itself, will help to symbolize and to exemplify the kind of competitive ferment that I have in mind. I have not hesitated, in certain instances, to indicate how I feel about the items I am listing. The reader is free, for the price of a postage stamp, to decide in every case if I am right or wrong.

BEST READING ON FREE SCHOOLS

Best five pages about Free Schools I have seen in print: Free Schools, by Frank Lindenfeld. Write: Vocations for Social Change, Box 13, Canyon, California, 94516. (Donations welcome.)

Best 300 pages about Free Schools, and one of the most eloquent and stirring books that ever has been written about education: *The Lives of Children,* by George Dennison. Vintage Books, 1970. ($1.95, paperback.)

Best regular, monthly information-interchange, with intermittent and often brilliant contributions by Mike Rossman, Peter Marin, Allen Graubard and Tim Affleck: *New Schools Exchange Newsletter,* 301 East Canyon Perdido, Santa Barbara, California, 93101. ($10.00 for one year.)

Best job-interchange for teachers who would like to work within the Free Schools, with loads of last-minute bulletins on new job openings in all sections of the country, summaries of important writings that appear in other journals and the warm, emphatic and responsible voices of its editors, Stan Barondes and Len Solo: *Newsletter of The Teacher Drop-Out Center,* Box 521, Amherst, Massachusetts, 01002. ($20.00 for one year.)

Newest and most careful listing of the Free Schools nationwide, with a detailed compilation of basic data on each item: *New Schools Directory,* 38 Kirkland Street, Cambridge, Massachusetts, 02138. ($1.25, paperback.)

Best in-depth background reading on the Free Schools and the struggle to "de-school" our own imagination and our own ideas on education; with some of the finest essays and informal pieces about Free Schools, politics and education to appear in any journal in the past five years: *This Magazine Is About Schools,* edited by Satu Repo, George Martell, Sarah Spinks and others who work in and out of Free Schools in and near Toronto. Write: 56 Esplanade Street East, Suite 301, Toronto 215. ($4.00 for one year.)

Best political news and commentary on the Free Schools, public schools, racism, children's rights, women's liberation . . . heavy emphasis on struggles taking place here in the Eastern cities: *Outside the Net,* edited by John Vanden Brink and Thomas Wilbur. Write: P.O. Box 184, Lansing, Michigan, 48901. ($4.00 for two years.)

Twenty-two Free School "models," all now in existence: "The Free Learner," a series of concise one-page descriptions of Free Schools, no two quite the same. Write: Constance Woulf, 4615 Canyon Road, El Sobrante, California, 94503. ($2.00, single copy.)

Leads and contacts for the Free Schools nationwide: emphasis on West Coast; organizing strategies; political consciousness; special issues on racism; health-care; housing; women's rights: *Vocations for Social Change,* written and assembled by a high-spirited collective based in Canyon, California, but keeping in touch with local groups in several major cities. Box 13, Canyon, California, 94516. ($5.00 for six months.)

CONTACTS AND CLEARING-HOUSES FOR THE
FREE SCHOOLS WEST TO EAST

Seattle, Washington, and the Northwest: Good writing, dialogue, concrete and specific issue-solving; a small informal publication: *Newsletter* of the New School Movement, 402 15th Street East, Seattle, Washington, 98102. (No charge.)

California
1. Education Switchboard, 1299 Fourth Street, Suite 308, San Rafael, California, 94503. (No charge for mail information.)
2. San Francisco Education Switchboard, 1380 Howard Street, San Francisco, California, 94901. ($2.00 for *Newsletter.*)

3. New Schools Network, 3039 Deakin Street, Berkeley, California, 94705. ($2.00 for *Newsletter*.)

Arizona, mainly Phoenix-Tucson area: Experimental Schools Corporation of Arizona, P.O. Box 2735, Tucson, Arizona, 85702. (No charge for mail information.)

New Mexico and other sections of the Southwest: Rio Grande Educational Corporation, 213½ West San Francisco, Santa Fe, New Mexico, 87501. (No charge for mail information.)

Oklahoma, Louisiana, Arkansas and Texas: Southwest Education Reform Community, 3505 Main Street, Houston, Texas, 77002. (No charge for mail information.)

St. Paul and Minneapolis: Street Academies and Free Schools: with detailed descriptions of several Free Schools now in existence in that area, including a description of the Urban League Street Academy of Minneapolis, by its Headmaster, John E. Doyle: *Education Explorer,* published by the Education Exploration Center, 3104 16th Avenue South, Minneapolis, Minnesota, 55407. ($2.00 for single copy of *Education Explorer;* $3.00 for *Newsletter* subscription.)

Milwaukee: Black, Spanish, Integrated Free Schools: Milwaukee Federation of Community Schools, an organization of seven parent-operated schools established in buildings previously occupied by Catholic schools and funded with preliminary assistance from the Catholic church. For background information write: Marquette University, Division of Continuing Education, 1217 West Wisconsin Avenue, Milwaukee, Wisconsin, 53233, and ask for *The Federation of Independent Community Schools.* (No charge for reprint.) For recent information write: The Federation, 2637 North 11th Street, Milwaukee, Wisconsin, 53206. (No charge for pamphlet.)

Chicago area: Two Free Schools with a good survival record and a lot of useful information about how they did it:
1. The Southern School, a small and remarkable school, serving primarily poor white children, created and directed by Pat Zimmerman. The original funding proposal is a model of effective, clear and stirring writing of the kind that gets the

money. Write: 4645 North Clark Street, Chicago, Illinois, 60640. ($2.00: only if you can afford it.)

2. St. Mary's Center for Learning, one of the most successful, longest-lasting and best-regarded Free Schools in the nation. For a copy of their budget, prospectus and fund-pitch, write: 2044 West Grenshaw, Chicago, Illinois, 60612. (No charge: send what you can afford.)

Illinois: Springfield, Evanston, Decatur, Champaign. Write: Carole Whitcomb, The New School, Route One, Oakley, Illinois, 62552. (No charge for mail information.)

St. Louis: Street Academies and Free Schools: One of the best-informed, most down-to-earth people in this movement: a man who was running an informal Street Academy way back in 1964, and is still in the same place, and is still doing the same thing. Write: Dennis O'Brien, LOGOS, 3325 Washington Avenue, St. Louis, Missouri, 63103. (No charge for mail information.)

Indianapolis: Street Academies and Free Schools. Write: John B. Kesterson, Community Organization Program, Eastside, 1258 Windsor, Indianapolis, Indiana, 46201. (No charge for mail information.)

New Orleans: The Innovative Education Coalition, 1130 North Rampart Street, New Orleans, Louisiana, 70116. (No charge for mail information.)

Washington, D.C.
1. Lots of detailed information about municipal regulations, accreditation, legal and extra-legal difficulties, strategies and detours: Washington Area Free School Clearing House, 1609 19th Street, Northwest, Washington, D.C., 20009. (Send one dollar if you can.)
2. Less of the legal and strategic, more of the political and pedagogic: Marcus Raskin, Institute For Policy Studies, 1520 New Hampshire Avenue, Northwest, Washington, D.C., 20036. (No charge for mail information.)

Baltimore: Free School Switchboard, 319 East 25th Street, Baltimore, Maryland, 21218. (No charge for mail information.)

Philadelphia, New York, Boston and points in between: A new, strong, broad-based information-interchange for the Free Schools in this section. Discussion and debate among active Free School people. Increasing black and Puerto Rican participation and with a solid emphasis on building mutual support among the Free Schools working with poor people. Write: Marge Hart and John Paternaude, *KOA Newsletter.* 2411 Lorillard Place, Bronx, New York, 10458. ($5.00 for one year.)

New Jersey: New Jersey Alternative School Foundation. Write: Terry Ripmaster, 16 Crestwood Drive, Glen Rock, New Jersey, 07452. ($3.00 for subscription to *Newsletter.*)

New York City

1. Funding practices, pedagogic hassles, decision-making, parent-teacher cooperation and administrative challenges of three well-known and successful schools. Write: Judith Macaulay, East Harlem Block Schools, 94 East 111th Street, New York, New York, 10029. (Donations welcome.)

2. How To Start A Free School in New York. Transcript of a forum held in winter, 1970. Lots of details about money, laws and Building Code. Write: *Summerhill Society Bulletin,* 339 Lafayette Street, New York, New York, 10012. (Fifty cents for single copy of the April, 1970, issue. For subscription to the *Bulletin:* $7.50 adults, $2.50 children.)

3. The Street Academies and Harlem Prep. *Carnegie Quarterly,* Fall, 1968, Carnegie Corporation, 437 Madison Avenue, New York, New York, 10030. (No charge for single issue.) For more recent information write: Edward Carpenter, Harlem Preparatory School, 2535 Eighth Avenue, New York, New York, 10030. (No charge for mail information.)

4. LEAP School: a strong, activist, street-centered, action-oriented learning-workshop on the Lower East Side of Manhattan. Several pieces of good, vivid, and eloquent documentation are available: *Street Kids,* by Larry Cole and several of the LEAP School students, Grossman Publishers, 1971. ($6.95, hardcover.) *Checking It Out,* by Michelle Cole and Stuart Black, Dial Press, 1971. ($5.95, hardcover.) *LEAP School Catalog 1971-*

1972, LEAP School, 540 East 13th Street, New York, New York, 10009. (Send $2.00 donation if you can.)

5. Summerhill Collective: a small activist collective which is involved in the fight for children's rights and serving also as a clearing-house for a limited number of Free Schools. Write: 137A West 14th Street, New York, New York, 10011. ($3.00 for *Newsletter* subscription.)

6. Children's Community Workshop School. An excellent description of this school, as well as of the New School of Decatur, Illinois, is included in Jane Howard's essay, which appeared first in *Life* Magazine. Write: Jane Howard, Editorial Department, Time & Life Building, Rockefeller Center, New York, New York, 10020. (No charge for reprint.)

Long Island: Long Island Free School Exchange, 55 Hartwell Place, Woodmere, New York, 11598. (No charge for mail information.)

Northern New York State: good contacts in New England and in New York City: Mary Leue, Albany Free School, 20 Oxford Road, Albany, New York, 12203. (No charge for mail information.)

Connecticut: A lot of candid and painful information on the agonies of getting started, finding money and organizing staff. Strong emphasis on racism, black studies, Puerto Rican studies, at the secondary level. Write: Philip Rose, South Norwalk Community School, 65 South Main Street, Norwalk, Connecticut, 06854. (No charge for mail information: send $2.00 donation if you can.)

Boston and Eastern Massachusetts

1. Jobs for teachers in the Free Schools in the Boston area: Vocations for Social Change, East Coast office, 351 Broadway, Cambridge, Massachusetts, 02139. (No charge for mail information.)

2. Information about Free Schools in Eastern Massachusetts: The Education Center, 57 Hayes Street, Cambridge, Massachusetts, 02138. (No charge for *Newsletter*: donations welcome.)

3. A strong piece of narrative description on the Highland Park

Free School in Boston by its first Headmaster, Luther Seabrook: *Social Policy*, May-June, 1970. Write: P.O. Box 534, Cooper Station, New York, New York, 10003. (No charge for reprint.)
4. Two related essays on Highland Park, The Storefront Learning Center, Roxbury Community School and The New School for Children: profile-in-depth of the four Free Schools in Boston, including interviews with Ken Haskins, Edward Yeomans, Harvey Haber. *City*, summer issue, 1971. Write: Urban Coalition, 2100 M Street, Northwest, Washington, D.C., 20037. ($2.00 single copy.)

URBAN EMPHASIS

The most knowledgeable and important black-oriented training-and-curriculum organization in the East. Information and direct consultation on the setting-up of Free Schools in a black or poverty community; black emphasis, parent control, community participation; films, curriculum materials, training and development of staff. The organization is black-run, black-owned and largely staffed with veterans of the schooling struggles in New York, Washington and elsewhere in the East. Write: Preston Wilcox or Kenneth Haskins, Afram Associates, 103 East 125th Street, New York, New York, 10037. (No charge for mail information.)

Another strong, New York-centered organization of those who have been involved in schooling and de-schooling struggles for the past ten years. Emphasis on the training of teachers who live in the neighborhood in which they teach, who share a political consciousness and who are devoted to community participation in the process of a child's education. Main concentration is on black and Spanish-speaking neighborhoods. Write: The Teachers, Inc., 50 Pike Street, New York, New York, 10012. (No charge for mail information.)

Information on the training of parents and in the organization of a parent-base to make decisions and to develop a sense of critical leverage in regard to choice of teachers, administration and the like. Write: United Bronx Parents, 791 Prospect Avenue, New York, New York, 10455. (No charge for mail information.)

Sound tapes of lectures and discussions by David Spencer, Preston Wilcox, Marilyn Gittell, George Dennison, Edward Carpenter, Rhody McCoy, Mario Fantini and a number of others who have been involved in the struggles of the Free Schools and the public schools of New York City. Ideal for provoking discussion and debate in parent organizations during the early planning-stages of the Free School. Write: Living Library Corporation, 211 Centre Street, New York, New York, 10013. (No charge for catalog: there is a charge for tape cassettes.)

Essays on political indoctrination, struggle and rebellion in the New York context, with the voices of Doxey Wilkerson, Marilyn Gittell and Charles E. Wilson, former Unit Administrator of I.S. 201: *Schools Against Children,* edited by Annette T. Rubinstein, Monthly Review Press, 1970. ($7.50, hardcover.)

The most searching piece I have yet seen on the inner political dynamics of a large and racially integrated Free School, Adams-Morgan School, in Washington, D.C., written by Paul Lauter; also several good pieces by Charles Hamilton, Florence Howe and Larry Cuban: *The Community and the Schools,* Harvard Educational Review, Longfellow Hall, 13 Appian Way, Cambridge, Massachusetts, 02138. ($3.50 single copy.)

Ann Carpenter writes on Harlem Prep; Michelle Cole on LEAP School; several other good pieces by Herbert Kohl, Henry Resnick, Peter Marin and Edgar Friedenberg: *High School,* edited by Ronald Gross and Paul Osterman, Simon and Schuster, 1971. ($6.95, hardcover.)

Black-run, black-conceived, semi-autonomous school experiment planned for 5000 pupils in Seattle, Washington, and scheduled to open in 1972. Write: John Little, Battelle Seattle Research Center, 4000 Northeast 41st Street, Seattle, Washington, 98105. (No charge for mail information.)

Independent school experiment intended for Mobile, Alabama,

now in the final planning-stage. Write: Vic Solomon, National
C.O.R.E., 200 West 135th Street, New York City, New York,
10030. (No charge for mail information.)

*Plan and proposal for a large and integrated urban Free School
with a neighborhood base and a political orientation:* "The
Newark Community School," by Eric Mann. It never started;
Mann, like Ayers, joined the Weathermen and turned entirely
to political action. It is dated now, but still an excellent blue-
print: *Liberation,* August, 1967, New England Free Press, 791
Tremont Street, Boston, Massachusetts, 02118. (Ten cents.)

*Description of an exciting learning-center begun and operated on
the corner of 129th Street and Madison Avenue in Harlem:*
candid details on the black-white difficulties: *The Storefront,*
by Ned O'Gorman, Harper, 1971. ($1.25, paperback.)

READING, HARD SKILLS AND CURRICULUM

Detailed lists of good materials and ideas from Bill Ayers, Wilbur
Rippy and John Holt: The final pages of *The Lives of Children* (see page 126).

The teaching of reading at the elementary level, a gentle, wise,
if somewhat dated book: *Teacher,* by Sylvia Ashton-Warner,
Bantam, 1964. ($1.95, paperback.)

Honest, unromantic and important passages on the teaching of
reading at the junior high school level: *How to Survive in Your
Native Land,* by James Herndon, Simon & Schuster, 1971.
($5.95, hardcover.)

An eloquent, brief but very important piece of writing, a little
book published several years ago but which, in a number of
respects, has helped to create the climate in which all of us
have been working ever since: *Teaching the Unteachable,* by
Herbert Kohl, New York Review of Books, 1967. ($1.00, paper-
back.)

The teaching of poetry by serious authors, many of whom have
had a good deal of experience in working with children in the

classroom: Teachers & Writers Collaborative, Pratt Center for Community Improvement, 244 Vanderbilt Avenue, Brooklyn, New York, 11205. (No charge for mail information.)

The writing of poetry, one of the best things on this subject I have read: *Wishes, Lies and Dreams,* by Kenneth Koch, Chelsea House, 1970. ($7.95, hardcover.)

Writing by children, and good, warm, personal advice from a man who has a rare and special grace with kids. Write: Richard Lewis, 141 East 88th Street, New York, New York, 10028. (No charge for mail information.)

Two good how-to-do-it books on the teaching of reading, by one of the very best and most down-to-earth writers in the country: *Hooked on Books,* by Daniel Fader, Berkley, 1968. (75 cents, paperback.) *The Naked Children,* by Daniel Fader, Mac-Millan, 1971. ($6.95, hardcover.)

The best phonics approach that I have seen for the teaching of reading. Square, straight, rigorous. It works. *The Writing Road to Reading,* by Romalda Spaulding, Morrow, 1969. ($8.95, hardcover.)

The two best books that I have seen on the political character of education, both of them directly relevant to the teaching of reading and to a number of the other issues raised within this book: *The Pedagogy of the Oppressed,* by Paolo Freire, Herder and Herder, 1970. ($5.95, hardcover.) Also, *Cultural Action For Freedom,* by Paolo Freire, Center for the Study of Development and Social Change, 1430 Massachusetts Avenue, Cambridge, Massachusetts, 02138. ($2.00, paperback.)

Books in Spanish: Downtown Book Center, 19 Southeast First Avenue, Miami, Florida, 33131. Quinto Lingo, Emmaus, Pennsylvania, 18049. Pan American Union, 19th Street and Constitution Avenue, Washington, D.C., 20006. For more concrete and more specific help: Phil Rose, listed under Connecticut (above). For the same, but with a more political orientation: Armando Martinez, PUENTE, 531 Massachusetts

Avenue, Boston, Massachusetts, 02118. (No charge for mail information.)

Math, science, other curriculum ideas: Elementary Science Study, E.D.C., 55 Chapel Street, Newton, Massachusetts, 02160. (No charge for mail information.)

Workshops in leather, photography, cardboard carpentry, etc., with people who also have a consciousness of the world that is not made of tri-wall and a considerable dedication to the struggles of the parent-groups within the cities: Workshop For Learning Things, 5 Bridge Street, Newton, Massachusetts, 02160. (No charge for catalog.)

Fractions, measurements, use of tape recorder in children's writing: good bits and pieces in pages 111 to 211 of *What Do I Do Monday,* by John Holt, Dutton, 1971. ($6.95, hardcover.)

Information and background on the development of a politicized course of study, including "The Vietnam Curriculum," of which she is co-author; also source for materials on education in the context of the total family: Joan Goldsmith, Newton College of the Sacred Heart, 885 Center Street, Newton, Massachusetts, 02158. (No charge for mail information.)

Two rich, exciting catalogs filled with many specific and provocative ideas for hundreds of different courses at the secondary level: *LEAP School Catalog, 1971-1972* (see above). *Catalog of Community Gamma,"* Parkway Program, The Franklin Institute, 20th Street and The Parkway, Philadelphia, Pennsylvania, 19103. ($1.00 for catalog.)

Binding, printing, publishing of children's books: George Cope, John Merrill, Nat Burwash and others. Teachers and kids can come and learn to do it on their own: E.D.C., 55 Chapel Street, Newton, Massachusetts, 02160. (No charge for mail information.)

Inexpensive versions of much of the material used in Elementary Science Study units (see above): Selective Educational Equipment, 3 Bridge Street, Newton, Massachusetts, 02160. (No charge for catalog.)

Leicestershire workshops for teachers in the United States: materials and detailed suggestions for the elementary-level Free Schools: Betsye Sargent or Edward Yeomans, National Association of Independent Schools, 4 Liberty Square, Boston, Massachusetts, 02118. (No charge for mail information.)

Information on the Infant Schools in England, as well on some of the significant school-experiments now being carried on in the United States; a collection of important essays: *Schools Where Children Learn,* by Joseph Featherstone, Liveright, 1971. ($2.45, paperback.)

Workshops on English Infant School approach in the New Jersey area: The Children's Center, 38 Franklin Street, Tenafly, New Jersey, 07070. (No charge for mail information.)

Helpers, boosters and advisers at all levels of education, but especially at the elementary level: David and Frances Hawkins, Mountain View Center for Environmental Education, 511 University Avenue, Boulder, Colorado, 80302. (*Newsletter* subscription free on request.)

A short, inventive, high-spirited handbook, of great use to Free School kids who want to study and dissect the workings of the public school across the street: *The Soft Revolution,* by Neil Postman and Charles Weingartner, Delta, 1971. ($1.95, paperback.)

Practical descriptions of some of the best new work from several experimental curriculum groups, including a precise and detailed description of "Chamber Theater," Carolyn Fitchett's very successful approach to the study of literature with high school kids: *Making New Schools,* by Joseph Turner, David McKay, 1971. ($5.95, hardcover.)

Detailed descriptions of numerous experimental programs in a number of widely separated sections of the country. I disagree with many of the generalizations offered in this book; it presents, nonetheless, a series of very accurate vignettes of a large number of educational alternatives which may be of use in helping to provoke ideas within the Free Schools. *Crisis In The Classroom,* by Charles Silberman, Vintage, 1970. ($2.45, paperback.)

A candid and important exchange of views on several of the issues which are raised within the pages of this book, in particular in regard to hard skills and the function of the teacher: "The Schools We Want: A Family Dialogue," by Margot and Nat Hentoff, *Saturday Review,* September 19, 1970.

A magazine of innovative resources for education. It has been in the recent years, a great deal more disposed to gadget-oriented resource-tools and to Zen mysticism than some of the political realities of the decade seem to call for. The issue of fall, 1971, edited by Skip Ascheim, is, however, something very special: *Big Rock Candy Mountain,* 115 Merrill Street, Menlo Park, California, 94025. ($8.00 for a year's subscription, $3.00 for the issue of fall, 1971.)

How children can learn by teaching one another, with descriptions of various programs in which children function as the teachers of their peers or of children who are younger than they are: *Children Teach Children,* by Alan Gartner, Mary Kohler and Frank Riessman, Harper and Row, 1971. ($5.95, hardcover.)

MONEY-RAISING, FOUNDATIONS, FEDERAL
GOVERNMENT, INCORPORATION PROCEDURES,
LEGAL HASSLES

Pat Zimmerman's funding proposal for the Southern School: see Chicago area (above).

New Nations Seed Fund: a small nonprofit trust established at the inspiration of George Dennison, administered by Judy

Thompson and dependent for its income upon kids and grown-ups in all sections of the country who donate fifty cents, a dollar or several dollars on their birthdays; money to be used, upon receipt of letter applications, to help to start or strengthen Free Schools which serve, at least in part, the children of poor people, and with the emphasis on elementary level. Write: Box 4026, Philadelphia, Pennsylvania, 19118. (No charge for mail information.)

Listings on almost 7000 trusts, foundations, corporations in the United States which possess assets of $200,000 or give away $10,000 or more annually; listings of special emphasis and special areas of concentration; names of directors and trustees; sources of wealth: *The Foundation Directory,* Russell Sage Foundation, 444 Madison Avenue, New York, New York, 10022. ($15.00)

Listings on much of the above, fund-raising sources, documents, etc., written in Spanish, for Spanish-speaking parents and teachers: *Recurso para Fundos,* New York City Training Institute, 214 East Second Street, New York, New York, 10002. Also available from Bay Tech Clearing House for Community Action, 1507 22nd Street, Northwest, Washington, D.C., 20007. (No charge.)

How to write a proposal for the large or middle-sized foundation; the best, most down-to-earth and least expensive handbook on this subject: *Seeking Foundation Funds,* National Public Relations Council of Health and Welfare Services, 419 Park Avenue South, New York, New York, 10016. ($2.50)

Federal funds: the most exhaustive source-book in existence. Descriptions of every Federal program which involves potential, direct or indirect funding for a Free School: *Catalog of Federal Domestic Assistance,* Superintendent of Documents, U.S. Government Printing Office, Washington, D.C., 20402. ($6.95)

Simplified breakdown on the Federal funding possibilities, with realistic advice on how to go about it: *Everyman's Guide to*

Federal Programs, New Community Press, 3210 Grace Street, Northwest, Washington, D.C., 20007. ($10.50)

Federal job-training programs, used by many Free Schools to pay parents and teen-agers to be trained as teachers and to work in the Free School at the same time. Write: Neighborhood Youth Corps, U.S. Department of Labor, Manpower Administration, 1726 M Street, Northwest, Washington, D.C., 20210. (No charge.) Also: New Careers Development Center, Room 238, School of Education, New York University, 239 Green Street, New York, New York, 10003. ($5.00 for subscription to *Newsletter.*)

Publicity, advertising, money-raising, proposal-writing, building-safety, legal hassles, anything else a Free School needs to know; the best not-for-profit consulting group I know: Duncan Yaggy or Harvey Pressman, VITA-Boston, 115 Gainsborough Street, Boston, Massachusetts, 02115. (No charge for mail information: expenses only for on-the-spot advice.)

How to set up a profit-making business to support a Free School: Charles Hampden-Turner, Center for Community Economic Development 1878 Massachusetts Avenue, Cambridge, Massachusetts, 02140. (Free assistance to any group which serves the children of poor people and which has some prototype significance.)

Building Code, trustees, incorporation, truancy law, certification and accreditation, sample documents of by-laws, articles of incorporation and the rest, information on the way to get free legal counsel; by far the most useful handbook on the legal hassles: *Alternative Schools, A Practical Manual,* Harvard Center for Law and Education, 38 Kirkland Street, Cambridge, Massachusetts, 02138. (Free.)

Building Code, trustees, certification and the like, including much of the above, but with the relevant details for the State of California: *New Schools Manual,* New Directions Community School, 445 Tenth Street, Richmond, California, 94801. ($2.00 for new edition.)

Vouchers, court suits, neighborhood suits, class suits, funding

strategies involving use of public funds to finance Free Schools;
also excellent advice on any of the legal difficulties: Paul Di-
mond, Harvard Center for Law and Education, 38 Kirkland
Street, Cambridge, Massachusetts, 02138; Steve Arons, 52 Rob-
erts Road, Cambridge, Massachusetts, 02138; Walt Senterfitt,
The Learning Place, 256½ Collingwood Street, San Francisco,
California, 40414. (No charge for mail information.)

*The best source of month-to-month information on voucher
struggle, legal issues, court suits and the like, involving Free
Schools, children's rights, etc.;* with a strong, partisan position
in behalf of social change and education activism: *Inequality in
Education,* Harvard Center for Law and Education. (Address
above.) Ask for numbers three and four, which include a long
and excellent piece about the Free Schools and alternative
schools throughout the nation, written by the new Headmaster
of Highland Park Free School, Charles Lawrence. (Subscription free.)

*The major source of new creative work and long-range strategies
for the voucher system,* as well as a lot of useful data on the
Free Schools: Kathy Woodward and Christopher Jencks, The
Cambridge Institute, 1878 Massachusetts Avenue, Cambridge,
Massachusetts, 02140. ($4.00 for full report on voucher study;
shorter materials, including reprints of some of Jencks' best
work, available for free.)

*Down-to-earth and practical suggestions concerning fund-raising,
politics and organization,* from one of the most effective organizers and fund-raisers in the nation: *The Professional Radical,
Conversations With Saul Alinsky,* by Marion K. Sanders, Harper
and Row, 1970. (Ninety-five cents, paperback.)

GOOD PUBLICATIONS FOR TEACHERS
FIGHTING IN THE SYSTEM

"No More Teachers' Dirty Looks," Bay Area Radical Teachers'
Organizing Committee, 1445 Stockton Street, San Francisco,
California, 94122. ($2.00 for four issues.)

"The Teacher Paper," a lively, irreverent, practical newsletter for teachers in the public system, edited by Fred and Robin Staab: 3923 South East Main Street, Portland, Oregon, 97214. ($3.00 for four issues yearly.)

"The Red Pencil," a good, radical, activist newspaper for teachers: Phyllis Ewen, 131 Magazine Street, Cambridge, Massachusetts, 02139. ($3.00 for subscription: also includes a bulletin issued once each month.)

BOOKS AND ESSAYS THAT HAVE BEEN OF IMPORTANCE TO ME IN THE WRITING OF THIS BOOK

De-Schooling Society, by Ivan Illich, Harper and Row, 1971. ($6.95, hardcover.)

School Is Dead: Alternatives in Education, by Everett Reimer, Doubleday, 1971. ($6.95, hardcover.)

Formative Undercurrents of Compulsory Knowledge, edited by Jordan Bishop and Joel Spring, CIDOC Cuaderno 1011, CIDOC, Apdo. 479, Cuernavaca, Mexico. ($6.95, paperback.)

Culture Against Man, by Jules Henry. Vintage, 1963. ($2.95, paperback.)

The Way We Go To School, by Larry Brown and The Task Force on Children Out of School, Beacon Press, 1971. ($2.95 paperback.)

Still Hungry in America, by Robert Coles, New American Library, 1969. ($3.95, paperback.)

Blaming the Victim, by William Ryan, Pantheon Books, 1971. ($6.95, hardcover.)

Health and Social Change: The Urban Crisis, by H. Jack Geiger, Lowell Institute, Boston, 1968. (No charge.)

Poverty and Mental Retardation: A Causal Relationship, by Rodger Hurley, Vintage, 1970. ($1.95, paperback.)

Let Them Eat Promises, by Nick Kotz, Anchor, 1971. ($1.95, paperback.)

NOTE: Additional documentation for those sections of this book which pertain to medical, social and educational discrimination are available to the reader upon request. Write: Education Action Fund (below).

TWO BOOKS, VERY DIFFERENT FROM EACH OTHER, AND VERY DIFFERENT FROM THIS ONE, BY PEOPLE ACTIVE IN THE FREE SCHOOLS

Rasberry Greenway Exercises, by Salli Rasberry and Robert Greenway. The authors are involved in a relatively isolated Free School, with little direct or obvious concern about the issues I have raised within this book. I cannot agree with their point of view, but they are serious and interesting people and have written a book which will be of great help to many people who are starting schools. Freestone Publishing Company, 440 Bohemian Highway, Freestone, California, 95472. ($3.00, paperback.)

Free The Children . . . The New Schools Movement in America, by Tim Affleck and Allen Graubard. An important, serious and comprehensive picture of the Free Schools nationwide, with a much broader focus and somewhat less partisan view than I have been able to present, but with lots of strong subjective viewpoints too, and food for many hours of good debate and disputation: scheduled for publication by Pantheon, autumn, 1972.

TEACHERS, FOUNDERS, DIRECTORS OF THREE OF THE EARLIEST FREE SCHOOLS

There are a half-dozen people whom I have known as close friends or co-workers and who seem to me to have a vast amount of detailed, practical and important information at their fingertips, not only in regard to curriculum and teaching methods and the like, but also in regard to internal struggles, political controversies and the struggle to raise money. The two individuals who seem most knowledgeable to me — and most realistic in the terms of hard survival — are Bernice Miller, first Headmistress of the New School in Boston, and Anita Moses, first Director of Children's Community Workshop in New York. I have referred to Mrs. Miller at several points within this book. Mrs. Moses is well known to people in New York. She is, simply, one of the most remarkable educators, organizers and good human beings I know. Both Mrs. Moses and Mrs. Miller are available for on-the-spot consultation in curriculum, organizing, money-raising and internal political struggles of the Free Schools.

Three of the original New School teachers — Nancy Verre, Joan Leonard and Melissa Tilman — have agreed to make available the experience they have gained to those who are just starting out as teachers in the Free Schools. Each in a different way is a brilliant and exciting teacher, and any Free School group would, I think, profit greatly from a day of workshops or just informal conversation with them. Gerald Friedberg, co-founder of Lorillard Children's School in Bronx, New York, is involved somewhat less with the urban schools right now, but nonetheless has a great deal of useful information to provide to those who are in need of practical advice in getting off the ground. Their addresses — and more details on their special areas of expertise — are available to readers on request. The addresses and special interests of several of the parent leaders named within the early pages of this book are also available to parent groups which are in need of practical counsel on the strategies and pitfalls of the first two years. Address the Education Action Fund below.

EDUCATION ACTION FUND

There are four packets of materials that my co-workers and I have put together from notes, jottings and correspondence during the past year:

(1) *Learning and teaching in the Free Schools:* Free School children write and publish their own books. Free School children examine and dissect the public school across the street. Free School children study tests, credentials, cumulative-records as the devices of control within the public schools. Free School children blitz the city with wall-newspapers. Free School children rent a billboard near the airport and give in-coming tourists unconventional advice. Free School children start their own block radio-station. Free School mothers, fathers and teachers learn to function in the classroom on an equal basis. Free School children learn how to open and to operate a pre-school.

(2) *Funding strategies:* the use of Richard Nixon's "Omnibus Crime Bill" to obtain the cash to subsidize a Free School in the Midwest. (Teachers and kids agree to identify themselves as "potential criminals" in order to qualify for Federal funds.) Pat Zimmerman's outline "How To Run A Benefit Concert and Take in Ten Thousand Dollars in One Night." Bea Miller's version of "The Backward Hustle."

(3) *Free Schools in the country that would like to join in strong and active partnership with people working in the cities:* shared salaries for teachers in two schools at once, combined classes, combined semesters, combined fund-raising ventures, exchange of school facilities for six-month sessions, other plans by which to bring good people in the country and the city into something more than token or symbolic ventures of cooperation.

(4) *Illich, Reimer and the debate about "de-schooling":* notes, letters, private papers and exchange of views between a number of Free School organizers, teachers, students, in the wake of the two important books by Ivan Illich and by Everett Reimer which have been published in the past two years. Implications of these writings for the direction and the tenor of the Free Schools.

The four packets, which change somewhat from month to month, total twenty-five to fifty pages. They are available for free. If you can afford it, please send a donation of five dollars, ten dollars or more, to subsidize the larger number of those who cannot pay for this at all. I would also like to plead with readers who are interested in obtaining more information about the Free Schools named within this book not to write or telephone these schools directly, but to forward letters through our P.O. Box. In this way, the Free Schools can carry on their work without a lot of interruption and will not have to go through the nightmarish business of trying to choose between the needs of their own children and the needs of well-intending strangers. The exceptions, of course, are Free Schools which have been listed by address.

My colleagues, Annette Holman, Jo Tackeff and I are going to revise this list of CONTACTS, LEADS, ADDRESSES in twelve months. We would be grateful to hear which leads pay off and which ones don't. We would also like to work in any new leads and ideas which readers want to recommend. We hope that this set of "Yellow Pages" will grow into a kind of dialogue between us.

EDUCATION ACTION FUND, INC.
Box 27
Essex Station
Boston, Massachusetts, 02112